Becoming Hummingbird

Becoming Hummingbird

*Charting Your Life Journey
the Shaman's Way*

Jane Galer

Poiêsis Press
Mendocino ManasotaKey

Poiêsis Press
Mendocino, California
www.poiesispress.com

The author acknowledges the intellectual property rights inherent to all indigenous peoples and in accordance with the *2007 UN Declaration on the Rights of Indigenous peoples, Article 11, 12, & 13*, agrees that use of spiritual, religious, and intellectual property by non-indigenous artists must be by permission only. The language and information contained in this book is developed from traditional knowledge and traditional cultural expressions of the Q'ero of Peru. The information is published with the full consent and permission of the Q'ero Elders. In addition, the author and Poiêsis Press voluntarily acknowledge the relationship between the author and the Q'ero people regarding the primary concepts upon which this book is written by sharing in profits and royalties derived thereof.

The author retains sole responsibility for the contents of this book and asserts her moral, artistic, and intellectual rights of protection.

ISBN 978-0-9845697-0-0

Back cover / interior art: Original illustration by Rebecca Matson Powers
Front cover: Nasca line hummingbird, public domain; stylization, Roo Harris

Printed on acid free paper.

Also by Jane Galer

poetry
Too Deep for Tears

The Spirit Birds

Outskirts

Forward & In the Dark

memoir
How I Learned to Smoke:
An American Girl in Iran

non-fiction
Spirit Dogs: How to Be
Your Dog's Personal Shaman

historical fiction
The Navigator's Wife

journal writing
Piecework magazine

Coreopsis Journal of Myth and Theater

EarthLines: The Culture of Nature

with deepest gratitude to

Don Porfirio Segueiros (Chino)
Don Francisco Chura Flores
Don Humberto Soncco Quispe
Doña Bernadina Apaza Flores

&

the Mountain of my Dreaming

Contents

Acknowledgments   xiii
Preface   xv
Author's Note   xix

My Hummingbird Journey   3

Part One   The Chakra Meditations   9
            Introduction   11
    1   Serpent   23
                The Serpent Meditation   25
    2   Jaguar   35
                The Jaguar Meditation   41
    3   Hummingbird   49
                The Hummingbird Meditation   54
    4   Eagle   61
                The Eagle Meditation   65
    5   The Lower World God   73
                The Huascar Meditation   80
    6   The Middle World God   91
                The Quetzalcoatl Meditation   99
    7   The Upper World God   105
                The Pachacuti Meditation   111

Part Two	Defining the Self	117
	Jung, Tarot, and Astrology	119
8	The Fool	127
	The Fool Meditation	132
9	The Magician	139
	The Magician Meditation	143
10	The Lovers	149
	The Lovers Meditation	155
11	Justice	161
	The Justice Meditation	168
12	The Twelfth Night	173
Part Three	Beyond Meditation	183
	Tarot and the Archetypes	185
	Conclusion: Tick Tock	193
Afterword		199
Additional Exercises		203
	Ancestor Retrieval	205
	Life Lines	209
	Destiny Tracking	
	Ninth Wave Meditation	211
	Altered States Simulation	213
Bibliography		215
Author's Biography		219

Acknowledgments

Becoming Hummingbird: Charting Your Life Journey the Shaman's Way would not exist without the initial encouragement and mentoring of Jo Bowlby, shaman and friend. Writing a book based on archetype meditations was her suggestion, and her involvement with the process of Becoming Hummingbird makes the project complete. Linda L. Fitch gave me generous encouragement and important early comments on the book and has continued to support me as a shaman and writer in the years since I was her student.

The critical member of my team is Diane Reynolds, who picks up all the pieces and assembles them exactly as they should be; nurtures me, directs me and entertains me in the way best of friends do. I also want to thank my personal support system, the love of my life, Gene, for always knowing the value of my work and for making my chosen life path smooth.

Thanks also to the critical companion of this life's journey, Barbara Saylor Rodgers; Karen Taylor for keeping me healthy and sharing this amazing path with me; Kristi Matson for grounding me in the world of poetry and giving of her extraordinary love. Thanks to Marilyn Long for her keen eyes reading manuscripts and her open heart, and a huge thanks to my writing mentors and friends, Robert McDowell and Medea Isphording Bern.

Preface

Becoming Hummingbird: Charting Your Life Journey the Shaman's Way
is a holistically driven approach to learning about and using mythology
and meditation to achieve a centered and productive spiritual life.
Composed of twelve guided meditations that take their form from
a combined essence of spiritual, Jungian, and mythological bases,
Becoming Hummingbird is an evolutionary method through which we
will attain insight into our truest life journey, our calling, our bliss.

The core plan of this meditation practice comes from my own
training with the Q'ero shaman of Peru and the energy medicine
teachers of The Four Winds Society. Within that teaching framework
we approached Jungian psychological understanding of archetypes in
new ways, using mythology and archetypes as mapping tools to bring
clarity to healing situations by taking them out of the mundane and
approaching them at the level of the sacred, the level of the gods, much
in the way Classical Greek mythology served the ancients as moral and
emotional guideposts. *Becoming Hummingbird* is also influenced by
Caroline Myss's ground-breaking work merging archetypal behavior
with Eastern concepts of chakras and astrology. Of course, Myss's work
was brilliantly and primarily an expansion of the concepts that form the
basis of Jungian psychology, and so this book has many attachments in
all of these worlds: integral philosophy, Jungian psychology, shamanism,
and both Eastern and Western cosmologies.

The question we ask is this. How do we make all of these complex
philosophies accessible to everyone? How do we offer a banquet of
mythological and cosmological choices to each individual whether they
come to the practice of meditation for the first time and without any
preconceived spiritual base or are longtime seekers on the journey of
Life? The answer is to offer a non-religious, widely accessible and earth-

centered menu in which the meditation itself offers an education, an enlightenment, and perhaps most importantly, a sense of the excitement of the first experience of deep awareness that comes from effective meditation practice.

Becoming Hummingbird's meditation format is not the blank slate of Zen meditation, it is not mindfulness, it is not supplicatory prayer in the common sense. It is an education in the mythology that has since recorded time assisted in the development of our spiritual selves, delivered in poetic form. Each meditation sets a mood of deep interrogation and personal expansion by offering touchstones to the archetypal and mythic traditions of the world. From the invitation of the meditative state we will chart our own journey, the mythic journey in the classical sense, whereby we identify our place, our goals, and our gifts.

This mythology of the Hero's Journey, the personal Grail Quest, is the universal story of how we each set a destiny and find our way. Although each of us has our own unique destiny and unique life to live, we are all on The Hero's Journey that begins, to use the vernacular of tarot cards, with The Fool and has as its final goal The World. We all struggle toward a perfect personal world against the same shadow archetypes, learning the same lessons, evolving toward the same goal of satisfaction. What is unique to each of us is the set, the pattern of positive traits and archetypes with which we design the specific pattern of our lives. Together these light and dark attributes weave our human story.

Becoming Hummingbird is composed of twelve meditations. Part One, including meditations One through Seven, relates directly to the seven chakras, or energy centers, of the physical body, and to the archetypes assigned to those chakras by the teachings of the Inka shaman. Here I have taken myth and unveiled the story to expose the life lesson, and then applied it to the physical realm of the body using the seven chakra system given to us by energy medicine. Working through these seven meditations as they appear allows the reader to develop his awareness of each energy center, its purpose, and the process of clearing required in order to be spiritually available for his finest destiny. Each meditation includes a discussion of the symbolism, an explanation of the way we understand and use that energy center/chakra, the meditation itself, an expansion of the mythology that makes up the core of the meditation, and an exercise for the reader to work through upon completing the meditation practice. Following through the chapter exercise prepares the reader to move on to the next meditation practice.

In Part Two, meditations Eight through Eleven relate to Jung's primal archetypes. Jung identified four archetypes that we all share in common: Child, Saboteur, Prostitute, and Victim. The four meditations in this section seek to transform those four primal archetypes, our baser selves, our "shadow" selves as Jung would say, into our destiny archetypes using the following four tarot card archetypal profiles that correlate to the Jungian base four: The Fool, The Magician, The Lovers, and Justice. These meditations are examples; they take our real world experience as self and by the transformative power of myth, propel it into the realm of the sacred. The tarot cards act as the catalyst. The meditations prepare the reader to develop her own destiny, her own unique and personal concept of the Hero's journey in what will be the twelfth and final meditation. Why twelve? Because this book of meditations might best be considered a year's guidance, a year of meditation in which your understanding of your singular life journey will unfold.

In the concluding section, we explore new ways to create myth from the basis of our own lives. The exercises in Part Three ask us to establish the work that is our life goal and find our place in the cosmos at large. The fundamental practice behind this work is shamanic, not psychological and not religious. The gift of the shamanic energy medicine work is its ability to transform for each of us, regardless of our belief system, the most basic questions we ask of our "self." Our aim is to leap beyond psychology, transcend religion, and evolve our understanding to new levels that connect us directly to the universal, to the sacred. The universe is asking us to actively participate in our own evolution. We have the opportunity to evolve genetically within a generation. The challenge is to open the pathways to our destiny and agree to explore them together.

Author's Note

I am grateful to the Q'ero shaman of Peru for making this incredible work accessible. Often during the course of our journey through these meditations I will refer to "my teachers" or "my teacher." I am speaking of the Q'ero shaman themselves, and of their Western students and teachers who also learned from the Q'ero and were encouraged to take those shamanic methods and philosophy to the wider audience, including in particular Linda L. Fitch, Alberto Villoldo, Wake and Kinlen Wheeler, Jon Rasmussen, Christine Paul, Jillian Vogtli, and Dean Taraborelli of The Four Winds Society where rigorous formal classes took place. Sometimes I'm not certain who said what first. Often what one or the other has said is a translation from the Quechua language spoken by the Q'ero. But since they, the Q'ero, the teachers, and the students work with this information as one, speaking with one voice, I have not cited them by name. In our shamanic work there is no hierarchy, we are all students, and we are all teachers.

Most importantly I would like to emphatically recognize the importance of indigenous peoples' intellectual property rights. During the time I spent with the Q'ero shaman in Peru I was able to ask permission of these Q'ero elders to write a book which would include some of their philosophy, cosmology and teachings. They were wholeheartedly encouraging of my project. While the debate over cultural and intellectual property rights grows in direct relation to how quickly our world is becoming accessible in all its most hidden parts, it is always of upmost importance to treat everyone's cultural heritage with respect and autonomy. The teachings of the Q'ero shaman who personally taught and influenced me has shaped my belief system. It forms the core of my philosophical actions, I am indebted to them for giving these gifts to the world.

Becoming Hummingbird

My Hummingbird Journey

Dear Reader,

I am deeply indebted to the shaman of Peru for bringing down from the mountains their incredible teachings. Chino and the Q'ero Don Francisco, Dona Bernadina, Don Humberto, led us to the mountains and shared their rich spiritual lives with us with grace, humor, equilibrium, and an honest desire to pass their traditions along to us. They are healers, spiritualists, ceremonialists, medicine men and women, and wisdom keepers. They are stewards of the earth.

I had a dream (no, really, stick with me for a moment on this). Before that I did a lot of searching, searching for a community of women who were interested in celebrating the esoteric, reviving the ancient feminine mysteries. I was looking for a connection, for *the* connection, for my spiritual roots. We gathered together. We worked with herbs, with ancient lore, we revived honoring customs that celebrated life passages. We touched each other deeply and kindled a fire that wanted to burn brighter. I began to seek more. What I longed for was a living tradition. Not a religion, not dogma and control, cult, clan or church; I was looking for ceremony that, once the connection was made, would come from within. Ceremony that wasn't done to me but by me. I had a craving for ritual that I have since seen time and again in the people around me. Life has had the ceremony neutralized out of it, drained of its life blood. I wasn't alone in my seeking. On a whim, my friend and I signed up for shamanic sessions during a much needed vacation in Big Sur. And life changed. Out of these sessions we learned about shaman classes based on the teachings of the Inka offered by an American school called The Four Winds Society. For months we debated signing up, extremely skeptical and wary. But the impact of our work with shaman Jon Rasmussen had so impressed us that we finally decided to try it. We could always quit, we could always just leave. We were not into "weird."

Six months later the first day of class came, a huge group of one hundred people, mostly women, mostly middle age like myself, and like women tend to do, most had come with a friend or two, so there were clusters of women chattering, with friendly, open faces. Very, very normal. The class began, the material was interesting, if a little too self-help-y for me but the beginning of anything is always a slow process, gearing up. The day ended with a ceremonial fire, a mesmerizing ritual of honoring led by the teachers, and then we following in our own simple beginning sort of ways, and what we found was that our simplicity didn't matter, the fire and the ritual were what mattered and in the fire, we were equals. This was the beginning.

That night I had a dream. In my dream, a man appeared dressed in Peruvian traditional dress, brightly colored poncho, knitted chullo hat, dark face with handsome lines and twinkling deep eyes. This man spoke to me in a language I could not understand as he took my hand and opened it flat beneath his own. Into my hand he dropped stars: gold and silver and blue, like a cascade of coins, all the while speaking to me.

The next day in class our teachers announced we were in for a treat. The Q'ero shaman of Peru had come to the US to attend a conference nearby, and they would be coming to do ceremony with us later in the week.

Three days later, we filed into the lecture hall, now calmed by candlelight and incense and soft meditation chant. We found chairs and settled ourselves down looking around at our teachers placed before us, beautifully and dramatically presented in full ceremonial dress, deep in prayer. One by one we presented ourselves before a teacher to receive our first rite, and then waited to sit our turn before the Q'ero. When my turn came and I sat cross-legged before one Q'ero elder, close enough at last to see his face in the pale and flickering light, I saw that it was the same man from my dream, and I knew this was the connection I had longed for, this was the lineage, the anchor, the tether that would ground my spiritual and energetic track in living work.

My calling to the shamanic path is not for everyone, but it is open to everyone, and from it comes some useful and universal truths. Whatever the path that led you to this book, you are welcome here, and whatever path guides you through life, you are blessed to have it as your own, for that path in itself is the first step. We are all wanderers, seekers. We thrive on ritual, and the spiritual part of our brains requires the food of ceremony. Being touched by ceremony is what brings otherwise composed people to their knees, brings tears to their eyes. Developing our personal ritual journey is what this book is about. In order to do that, we must learn about ourselves in possibly new ways.

In 2008, I spent time with the Q'ero in the Sacred Valley of Peru, daily working with them, in ceremony, hiking the mountains, camping, days and days with them in an intimate group. Their lives are in transition. They spend part of their time high in the Andes in their Q'ero villages, farming, helping their community as traditional healers. Then they come down to the valley, down to the towns and cities, and interact with modern Peru. In Cuzco they see clients seeking healings just as their own villagers seek them out. They work with Westerners like ourselves whenever asked to, that is part of their tradition, a shared lineage, open to all. In all of their day-to-day life what is spectacular is that the tradition, the ritual, is alive every single minute of the day. It's not reserved for Sunday morning, or before dinner, or bedtime prayers. It is in each moment, the sweetness of the hummingbird, a constant journey. They have an awareness of the earth as their mother and their place upon her that is profound. They know the meditative peacefulness that Buddhist monks exhort us to seek out. It's in their eyes, their smiles, every lighthearted or serious action they take.

I asked them, "Why?" Why are they teaching us, since it really does feel a little incongruous, as Westerners—we are always so eager. Their answer? Because you can help yourselves with this. Help each other. Help the earth. Don Humberto would spread out his hand across the earth in front of him in a characteristic gesture and a smile that said, "Why not?" in an "isn't it obvious?" sort of way.

Don Humberto reads the coca leaves. Coca leaf reading is technically rather like tea leaves…a form of divination, but unlike tea leaves it is not a party entertainment, coca leaf reading is serious. It can be exhausting. It is reserved for important issues, for destiny. Don Humberto speaks only Quechua and so conversation with him runs through a gauntlet of translation. Don Humberto reads the leaves for me, and what he tells me is that my future holds two books, that's my work. When I tell him about *Becoming Hummingbird* he just nods, like I'm not telling him anything he didn't already see in the leaves. I am humbled and honored to take this work and hold it fast in my heart. I do it for them, I do it for us, for you and me.

Con Munay,
Jane Galer

Part One

The Chakra Meditations

Introduction

In the traditional definition from Jungian psychology, archetypes are roles or original patterns of behavior "collectively inherited." In the Greek: *Archétypos* means first mold. Throughout time archetypes have been models for patterns of behavior shown through the telling of myths. These myths often recount an archetypal journey or quest, and they are tales from which we derive lessons about how to make our own journey through life. We have come to know these stories as Hero myths. *Myth* in its original definition in the Greek *Mythos* meant "story, word, speech" but did not imply truth or falsehood, fairytale or fiction the way it might today. Myths are the storyline through which archetypal patterns and their lessons are shared, every culture has them and in each culture these archetypes are similar; the common bond between all of man is the sharing of these universal traits.

Pioneer depth psychologist Carl Jung told us that we all have common behavioral bonds, or aspects, to our core personalities. He called these core modes of being "archetypes" and in doing so honored the ancients and the development of mythology as wisdom keeper. Mythology is the repository of archetypal history. It is where we go to find the correlative pattern for everyday behavior, the map, if you will.

Jung identified four basic core archetypes as: Victim, Prostitute, Child and Saboteur. We all embody either a dark or a light side, or sometimes both at once, of each of these modes of being. Just ask yourself, what do you sacrifice every day in order to get where you need to go? Prostitute. When did you last resort to pouting? Child. These are simplistic examples, but we can examine our lives and identify these four modes of being fairly readily.

Caroline Myss, prominent energy medicine teacher, did something wonderful. To Jung's core four aspects, she added eight more. These eight are fluid, changing, or open to change, and we can learn a lot about ourselves by understanding these eight personal archetypes and by occasionally revisiting them to see how we are learning, evolving, and improving our path. We can look and see if our Queen is a benevolent one or if we cling to being Queen because we are control freaks who need to let go, let in, or even let it out!

You don't need to care about Jung, archetypes, or self-help to benefit from a quick assessment of your own twelve archetypes, and to do that I highly recommend working through the process developed in Myss's book *Sacred Contracts* (Random House, 2002).

Our connection to the divine, to the sacred, is made by way of our own personal archetypes (the light and shadow of our personalities) and what we might perhaps label The Archetypes. Over centuries, since the dream time, mythology has been told and retold, and out of this mythology we find repeating patterns. These patterns are clues to the path of the hummingbird: the great journey of life, the Grail Quest, the seeker who seeks the divine, who seeks grace. These myths are rather unfortunately named, since myth, in our general use of the word, implies fiction. But the word "myth," "mythos" in the ancient use of it, meant the telling of a story as opposed to the acting out of a real event "logos," but the word itself never implied fiction. If we look at mythology and how it repeats in culture after culture, time after time, how it serves to instruct us about the path to grace, we see that the story the clues are cloaked in is fictive, but the path is true in the truest of ways. Mythology instructs us in the great universally understood patterns of life. And in every culture, every mythology's particular language, we see that these patterns are duplicated. They are archetypal emblems of the cycles of growing, questing, and being.

A lovely way to be introduced to these Archetypes is through the Greek myths. Here we find all we need to know about success and failure in life. Another place the archetypal journey is played out is in the Major Arcana cards of a tarot deck. In fact, some card readers like to read their spreads only in terms of the journey of the Hero toward enlightenment beginning with the first card, The Fool, and ending with the last, The World, the theory being that we all must work through each of the archetypes in order to complete our earthly cycle. Where the shuffled and selected cards fall shows our progress or regress in this universal quest. The Holy Grail is an archetypal trial.

What does this have to do with hummingbirds? For the Q'ero shaman of Peru, the hummingbird represents the collective lineage–all of the grandmothers, grandfathers, ancient spirits who bring wisdom down to us through the ages. Hummingbird is the journey in the form of the totemic animal guide. To become Hummingbird we are asking ourselves to find our place in this great long chain of being. The creation tales of the great Northwest Coast tribes are lessons about our connections between species and with the gods and the earth. The Inka show us the archetypes through animal spirits and multifaceted gods. These traditions have at their core the idea of balance and harmony within the journey. The lesson is that this is a matter of survival.

Our aim is to let the archetypes teach us to live like Hummingbird: optimally, energetically, with sweetness and patience, fierceness and longevity. The journey cannot be counted in days, but rather in moments of sweet nectar from the gods. When we become Hummingbird we no longer speak of "me" but rather see the universe from the broader perspective of "we" at all times. As Hummingbird, we map the great journey and we learn to master time. When we do this, everything, every moment, becomes sacred. This is our goal.

And so, how do we connect our own personal archetypes with the ones that are guideposts for The Journey? Through meditation.

How we come to the place of meditation or prayer is much the same process even though the goals of each might be different. Meditation and prayer help us step out of our own story and into ceremony and ritual. When we elevate consciousness to the level of ceremony, we begin to work at the level of myth and connect with Spirit, the unnameable energy of the sacred. On the other hand, if we sit around talking or concentrating glumly on our problems, we become stuck in Victim, stuck in the telling of our own stories rather than connecting to the great story of Spirit and the quest for grace. Therefore, we always work in a setting of ritual. Ritual and ceremony function as the catalyst that flips us out of the realm of the personal and into the realm of the sacred. Ceremony done by oneself is just as powerful as that done in a congregation of two thousand, perhaps more so, since when you're working alone your energy doesn't have to do battle with the energy of the woman sitting next to you who is really just planning her next shopping trip or fuming from an argument with her hubby. Meditation is your solitary ritual. Do it with all of the care and mindfulness that you would your own wedding, however simply or elaborately you might wish, but with intent. Think about what the word sacred means to you. What do you hold dear? How many ways do you already perform small sacred rituals each day, each season, each year? Every year I wait for the early spring day when I hear the song of the first returning thrush. That day I stop what I am doing and thank the earth for her amazing cycles of joy. I spend a little time outside, welcoming the thrush back into my life for yet another summer. We all have holiday rituals that have moments of the sacred attached to them, no matter how blurred and mundane they might sometimes become. The more ritual you can effect in your life on a daily basis, the more you will become aware of the consequences of your broader life journey. If even for a moment in an otherwise hectic day you create sacred space and honor the hummingbird within, you will notice very quickly that the journey carries more sweet seconds to it than it did before.

The Chakras

There is a shamanic relationship between the energy centers we widely call chakras and the archetypes. Most of us would agree that we have seven chakras, or possibly eight or nine depending upon the tradition you are following to learn about them, but for our purposes we will stick with the seven that relate directly to your physical body. In many indigenous cultures these centers of our energetic organization have identifying realms, areas of our being and behavior over which that center rules. In some Asian traditions these are called "chakras." In the South American shamanic traditions they are often called "ojos des luz," eyes of light, or "pukios," light wells. We can see that the concept of these energy centers has developed in various cultures over time and independently from each other, and yet the concepts are the same. We can often relate illness to these centers and certainly emotional turbulence. The best and most obvious example is the Heart Chakra (the fourth), but consider also the third which rules your gut instincts, your ego, and to which we can ascribe the expression "feel it in my gut." From the standpoint of mythology, each of these chakras has a ruling archetype. The four lower chakras are our physical nature and ruled by mythological power animals who, when layered from baser to more elegant, bring about our human nature.

The three upper chakras represent the worlds: Lower, Middle and Upper. Imagine a great tree, the roots of the tree run deeply below the surface, our unconscious realm; the trunk of the tree is right here before us, in this world of everyday reality, while the upper branches reach skyward to the stars, the super-conscious, our connection to Spirit, to the things that we have yet to know and to those things that are unknowable. These three higher chakras are ruled by gods, or the archetypal god forms that have been crafted for us through the ages in mythology so that we may learn all of god's forms and lessons.

The archetypal forms within each chakra that I will describe derive from the wisdom of the Inka shaman who happen to be my teachers, but this same wisdom comes down to us in the stories of the Sami in Siberia and the Native American in Alaska and in the Celt in Ireland. Sometimes the animal changes, but the mythology—the spirit of the animal's message—does not. For the Q'ero, the Hummingbird is our opportunity to taste the sweetness of life's journey, even though it is long and hard. In Europe there are no hummingbirds, but there is the crane, a bird that works just as hard at having the best life possible, is patient and knowing; perhaps, the crane is a better archetype in that setting. Or maybe a bird isn't appropriate at all and in Europe a wild horse will best represent the long journey. What matters is that the meditations for these archetypes take you out of your own story and into the great mythology that propels us forward into the future of our dreaming while tethering us back to the connection with Spirit that brings us on the journey at all.

The meditations in this book are introductions to the world of myth. They are meant to invite you to step away from your own story, give yourself over to the Quest, the hummingbird's journey. The meditations are not long, but they contain many names and references, some will be new to you, some will be old friends, guides you have long used. They are meant as a sort of catalog of mythology. As you work through the meditations, notice who calls to you within each meditation. You will begin to develop relationships with significant images and archetypes, and over time it is likely a single guide will appear in a meaningful way over and over again. Later, you will want to work with just this one name. Who is it, what is their wisdom, what tradition holds them as sacred, and how can they help you on your own journey? Do a little homework and expand what you know about that story. You will probably find that something within that specific myth is wisdom that fits perfectly into your life and how you have chosen to live it.

How to Begin

This book of meditations is laid out in such a way as to provide a method of study to be processed over the period of a year, twelve meditations. Although it is entirely up to the reader to settle into a rhythm with the work and define their own process according to their own personal needs, here are some suggestions for arranging the work. How you organize your meditation, and how often you go through the exercises and the meditations themselves is up to your own sense of your self. There may be some chapters that you work through quickly, others you may want to return to or linger over until you feel complete and ready to move on.

In general, you will want to read through the chapter once in order to get a sense of the focus and of the kind of work you will enter into for the month. This initial "research" period will allow you to assemble your altar materials, record the meditation onto your iPod and plan your month. Often we like to work from full moon to full moon, ending a month of work with a celebratory ritual fire, but we all have busy schedules and keeping to a rigorous notion of have-to's and process requirements doesn't work for any of us, so give yourself some leeway. If you can finish your month at approximately the same moon cycle each time, so much the better! Perhaps you like to work from new moon to new moon and take advantage of that period's energy and optimism to move you forward. Perhaps you appreciate the solemnity of the dark moon or the full moon's drenching power. Set a schedule that allows you to be flexible and yet still complete the work. The day before or the day after a full, new, or dark moon works just as well as the instant itself. Once you do set a schedule, try to stick to it.

Each chapter is a little bit different, each requires some preparation, some ceremony, and some "homework," and each will resonate with you in a little bit different way. As you work through the month you will want to immerse yourself in the characteristics of the archetype of the moment. In the initial meditations, where we are addressing the archetype and its connection to a chakra, you will want to spend your time taking on the mantle of that archetype and how it functions within its energy center. You will want to establish your altar first, perhaps spending a few days thinking about and arranging the altar, opening up the altar to your energy, and making a connection that is in its own way alive and active. Then, pick your day for ceremony and perform the meditation. Follow through with the exercises given, and complete the month of work with continued consciousness within the framework of the archetype. Reread the descriptions and notice how your understanding of the archetype has changed since doing the work. Dismantling your altar should be ceremonial, a closing. If you are incorporating ritual fire, finish the month with a transitional fire, thanking the fire for the month preceding but also asking the fire for energy toward the next month's work.

How much of each day you spend working with the material in each chapter will depend upon how significantly that archetype resonates with you, upon your own personal schedule, and upon your curiosity. At some point you will find yourself intrigued by the mythology and you might spend a very busy month researching further into the lore, spending many hours with your altar. These months may contain momentous revelations about your present journey, about your past. Other months might seem easy, obvious, or even superficial, and as long as you are sure that you aren't hiding from doing your work, you might breeze through the meditation without too much conscious effort.

Begin a journal where you will keep track of the insights you find within the meditations, work out the exercises at the end of the chapters, and take notes on your progress. It is essential to write down your thoughts after a meditation process. Altered states of consciousness are hard to recall. Try to make time for your journal as soon as you can after a meditation. You'll be surprised at how hard it is to remember what was, at the time, an earth shaking experience!

It's perfectly appropriate to do a meditation more than once if you feel you need to. You will also find additional exercises at the end of the book. If you are having trouble getting through a chapter, try adding an exercise. If you are excited by a chapter in particular, expand upon the work with added journaling and supplemental exercises.

Try to spend a part of each day working the archetype. What do I mean by that? Without giving in to the temptation to just *think* it out, try to immerse yourself in the qualities of the archetype. If you are, for example, working in Serpent in the first chapter, you are essentially shedding your past. It's visceral. You will become a sensory being, concentrating on how it *feels*. Peeling away, letting go, shedding. Your work of the month is heightened awareness of the physical realm. Each day should bring some increased sense of your body and its place in and on the earth. You might deliberately create time to bring your awareness to this first chakra connection, or you might just let it *be*—the approach has to be yours to define or it will not resonate as real. The material provided in the chapters is your menu of the options. Part of the work is for you to define the path in such a way that you are completely at ease with the process. If there is ever a moment when you say to yourself, "Oh, I don't know..." then you are straying off your path and doing what someone else wants you to do. You know those green witch books that want you to spin around three times and clap your hands seven times and spit sideways and in the middle of it you stop and say, "What?" It doesn't work because it doesn't come from within yourself. Your first meditation month will be a month of acclimation, finding what works, what's right for you. This is a very personal process.

Can you work through it at a faster pace? Of course. But personal experience has shown me that if you do the processes faster, you may end up having to repeat them, so take your time, and know that you will do the work in exactly the right amount of time, and in the way that is right for you, because that is what it is all about.

The Meditation Space

Before you approach your meditative space ready to do the practice, set it up. If you are doing this for the very first time it will take some effort and resourcing to assemble the right combination of things for and about your altar space. Give it some thought, this too is ceremony. We want to learn that ritual is a vibrant part of our active self. Eventually, in everything we do in any given day we will bring with us a sense of connectedness and ceremony, a sense of the sacred. How you assemble a sacred place in your consciousness and in your physical space is up to you, but bring to the process a heightened awareness, invite the universe to join you in your work.

If you can dedicate a room or an area of a room that will be undisturbed except when you are doing your meditative work, so much the better, but it's not required. Most of us want a space inside our private living areas that is dedicated, a place you can return to on a daily basis, but you could just as well plan to always do your process under your favorite tree or at the beach. Collect the basic ingredients: an altar surface, candles, essential oil diffuser or incense (be careful to purchase only high quality incense and pure essential oils). Assemble your icons: photos, statues, fetishes, beads, shells, feathers, leaves. These ornaments for your altar should reflect your current mood and will change over time and with each of our guided meditations. Don't clutter your altar with material things for their own sake, even a fetish should represent a current connection to the sacred, not just represent your favorite pet. Each month will require you to adjust your altar, adding or subtracting images and symbols. Make your altar a habit, present yourself before it daily, even if only to light a candle for five minutes while you drink your morning coffee. It will become an extension of your energetic self.

The sacred bath is an ancient ritual cleansing. It encompasses more than just a cleaning of the body. Islam uses bathing prescriptions in its prayer format. Novitiate nuns perform ritual hair cutting and other physical representations of their movement into the sacred space. Your personal sacred bath is setting the tone for the meditation to come. Soaking in Epsom salts scented with essential oils is relaxing for the body and calming for the mind. Light candles and begin your breathing process here if you like. Think of the bath as the place where you leave the world and its attendant worries behind. Instead of preparing yourself for a lover, you are the beloved. Afterward, perhaps you can slip on comfortable yoga wear or a loose robe and move barefooted before your altar.

As always, meditation works best when you are in a quiet space, a comfortable place, possibly with darkness around you. Light candles, smudge the room and yourself with sacred smoke, incense; doing this shows your awareness of the energetic dimension of your world. Cover yourself with something you have chosen specifically for this purpose, a shawl or quilt, and besides, you might be chilly while you sit. Everything you use should be chosen with intent, with sacred purpose. You might want to pair up with a friend and take turns guiding the meditation, or play a recording of the meditation in your own voice so that when you do enter the softened state of trance you can devote yourself entirely to the world presented to you. (If you have an iPod or MP3 player, prerecorded meditations are available for download at www.becominghummingbird.com.) Before you begin, spend several minutes cleansing your mind with deep breathing. Only begin the meditation when you know that you can devote yourself to these moments of deep space. All meditation is sacred behavior. Every step of it should be done with intention. You are calling grace from within your own consciousness and connecting to Spirit.

Don't forget to breathe.

Serpent

On the Belly of the Mother

Because our chakras are organized from bottom to top, lesser evolved to highest, and working through them in succession is a means toward working through and understanding ourselves—our "selves"—we will begin at the beginning. Adam, Eve, and—you guessed it—The Serpent! Actually, you can right now forget about Adam and Eve; they aren't the important ones in this story. It's the Serpent that counts.

What do we know about our first chakra? It is located at the root of the body, the base of the spine, the perineum. We identify it with our tribe, our grounding on this earth in this lifetime. Our life-force begins here. Basic survival. If your first chakra is weak you are perhaps not very comfortable here on Earth, can't come up with a sense of "home" or belonging, and suffer from the feeling that you might be born into the wrong family. Or you might feel you have an overactive "fight or flight" response, you strike out first and ask questions later—your first chakra is overpowering the others.

The military works from serpent, from the idea that the collective past needs defending, the military becomes a subculture stuck in first chakra sensation: kill or be killed. Other cultures through history and in many areas of the globe today are working out their issues in the first chakra; Rwanda is an example where the tribal connection was insincere and false to begin with. Even as we struggle to unite cultural stories into a world consciousness, we feed our first chakra tendencies to defend our individual tribes, and thus our differences flare up. When we only view the world from Serpent level we forget how to transform our baser connections into the mythic elegance of Hummingbird, where the journey is solo and chaos has been replaced by grace.

The Q'ero shaman of Peru say we worship at two altars, a golden one, the collective altar, and a silver one, our private personal altar. If you always follow the collective altar you are following someone else's set of instructive reasoning, someone else's path. We want to create our own altar, meaning that we want full control of our consciously and unconsciously created destiny. If we have created our personal destiny with integrity we will connect to the collective altar in the best possible way.

The Meditative Space

As I've said before, preparing your space is also a ritual. Choose a new candle for each meditation. Remake your altar in honor of the archetype or area of the sacred you will be working with. Use something special, a shawl or quilt that over time will, on its own, signify a meditative state the moment you throw it around your shoulders. Choose a soothing cleansing incense or aromatherapy scent. Take a sacred bath. In time this won't seem like a lot of work, it will seem like a part of the joy of stretching out the sacred hours available to you.

The Serpent Altar

Light a candle. Prepare your meditation space. If you have a snake totem or a symbol of the snake, put it beside the candle. You have just made a mini altar. She will be glad of that. Now be comfortable and breathe. When you're ready, read the meditation slowly, and always, always read it out loud.

The Serpent Meditation

She is Sachamama, the mother of the South wind,
she is unblinking and sightless.
Her tongue tastes the Earth's story in the air.
She rides the belly of the Mother, circling,
gliding, shimmering in palest light.
She is all hunger, seeking, wanting,
brightest color,
yet you cannot see her until she moves
because you touched her.

She will help you shed your past
just as she sheds her skin,
free of scars, of the old and unusable.
A ripple convulsion, and another,
her paper-thin scales shedding all in one piece.
She is an invitation to rebirth,
she is the pure energy of the creative, the life giver.

She is known by many names:
Hydra the water dragon,
many headed and elusive.
She is Wadjet, protector of women in childbirth.
She is Zu, the arch-serpent of the waters,
of the underworld.
She is Tiamat of Babylon, serpent of chaos,
when Marduk cut her in half
she became the sky and the earth.

She is of the oceans and seas
and known by many as Papohis.
She is Azhi Dahaka, creator of all the planets,
and she is Illuyankas, the divine.
She is Anyiewo the Rainbow Serpent,

the one who grazes on the rain,
her reflection is the rainbow in your sky,
the sound of her name is a wailing.
She is Uraeus,
and she lies within your spinal cord
connecting you to the sacred above and below.
Feel her moving up your vertebrae.
She is fertile and coils above your pregnant belly.
She is the healer, within and without, twined.
When she eats herself
she shows you the world never ending.
When the world turns right again,
she will assist us in shedding the old ways.

Follow her, she will lead you back
back to the garden.
She knows only the earth,
she holds it always along her entire body,
she walks the beauty way,
the way of pure sensation
the way of non-doing, non-suffering.

She is all of your senses, sight, touch, taste, smell.
See her, touch her, taste her, smell her. Be her.
Serpent, feel her coil within you,
within your belly, up your spine,
sliding slowly, determined, connected,
from your base to your throat,
fill yourself with her, with her power to heal,
to shed, to defend the Mother.

Shed as she sheds, convulsing,
glistening new skin.
Your awareness is bright like the sun,
you can feel everything through your new skin.
For a moment you are blind
blind as the skin covers your eyes,
a paper-thin veil of yourself as your past slides by,
now misty, now forgotten.

Convulse.
Heal. She is your backbone.
She comes out of the earth to bring you
to the garden, to wisdom.
Breathe and follow her.
Close your eyes and shed your skin.

When you have finished reading the meditation, sit in stillness and experience Serpent within yourself. Where and how do you feel her? Breathe. Be all sensation and dreaming. Give yourself time to experience the fire of your first chakra and the archetype of serpent within. As you emerge from your meditative state, bring serpent with you. Take a few minutes to readjust, ground with food and drink, and relax while you record your thoughts in your journal.

Where do you belong?

Some of us know the answer to this without even a thought. I'm Irish, or I'm a New Yorker, or I'm from Chicago. The rest of us might feel a little bit connected to our birth place, feel nostalgia for a small hometown. A small number of us feel nostalgia for less associative concepts like weather. I love and long for autumn. I don't feel connected to any place, or at least I didn't until I visited Ireland; suddenly I knew my homeland as if it were in my blood and genetic code, which it was. It's a good assist to the work of your first chakra to think about where you call home. Your rootedness, your true center on earth, where is it? If you can, make a pilgrimage to this place and perform an honoring ceremony. This is your starting off point, this is where Hummingbird begins her journey. This is the point from which you have thrown out a line to the magnificent destiny you are living in this lifetime. If you can't actually go to this place (and it should be a place, we're talking ground here after all), then perform a ritual using photos or memorabilia about that place, call it back into your first chakra and thank it for giving you stability, gravity. Write about it in your journal.

The Archetype of the Serpent

What is the practice hidden in the first chakra that the serpent archetype will extract for us? It is first and foremost to release the past. Forgive and forget might be the two most important acts of your entire life. They might also be the most difficult acts for you to accomplish. That's why you have Serpent to work with. One of my teachers says it's the greatest gift to have a physical body in which to work out our stuff. But it is also true that if we don't do the work, it is our physical body that will suffer. Our shamanic prayer for opening sacred space says "Shed the past, the way the serpent sheds her skin." How much clearer can it be? We're all stuck with some portion of Jung's Victim archetype, but we don't have to embrace it as our most thriving aspect. Give up your old stories. The work you do here, in the first chakra, prepares you to challenge and transform the shadow archetype of Victim when you approach the meditation for Justice later on in your work.

How? For a time, let's say one full moon cycle, try being Serpent. Everything is about the physical senses. So it's not "how" it's "what." What do you feel in your body, what does it feel like to live on the earth at this moment in time, right now without any history, any baggage, preconceptions or emotions? What is the nectar available to you from the Earth herself today? What is your body's response? What do you smell? Taste?

Release the old stories of your past, give them up to the Serpent and for a moment be blind and unremembering and then recall the rainbow and the glistening of new skin and be prepared to move forward. Serpent is about the basic, uncomplicated part of your brain/body response system. It requires no thinking, no emotion, no attachment to that skin of the past. Serpent is about reducing everything to its lowest primal response. Basic drive.

The Mythology of Serpent

The story of Adam and Eve might be the most prominent serpent tale we all know. Or do we? Do we remember that what the serpent said is that if we eat from the tree of knowledge we will know the difference between good and evil, and that therefore, we will be equal to God? The Serpent gave Eve a chance at godliness and she took it, but when she was challenged about her decision she placed blame rather than taking responsibility for her quest. The Serpent is the opportunity to take another step on the journey that Eve began on our behalf. Take responsibility for your quest and move forward along the archetypal path.

The Babylonian myth involving Marduk and Tiamat makes serpent into a near dragon-like monster. There is a common theme of gods in power struggles throughout mythology. In this case the struggle is between the most basic of states: will chaos reign or will order prevail and light the way? Marduk, a god similar in style to Zeus (an Olympian god), must slay the creature in order to gain power and control. He is the archetypal dragon slayer. Tiamat is the dragon, the sea serpent, mother of the gods and a creature of the earth's depths. She is an arch-serpent because she precedes god. (God in this context is the principle which brings order.) Therefore, she is also Chaos. Her role in the creation story is that of initiator; she is random potential. Being killed and cut in half by Marduk, her body became the sky and the earth, thus order birthed out of Chaos. By separating the worlds in this ordered way, the confusion the serpent causes by being of the earth and also on the earth is controlled. But notice that all creatures on the earth are wary of serpents even now. Their power for chaos is strong magic.

Many of the serpents of mythology were sea serpents and most were identified as representing the state of chaos from which the known world is born. In ancient times, the vast oceans represented danger and the unknown. Any creature dwelling in the ocean was powerful and fearful. Zu, a Sumerian serpent god also dwelled in the waters at the crossroads between life and death. Zu is another arch-serpent, and so, some element of Zu as being the archetype from which all other serpents derive has come down to us through time within this mythology. And while Zu is the mega-creature for a continent of peoples, we find arch-serpents rising up in nearly every other indigenous culture with knowledge of snakes. The repeated connection of the serpent form with life-giving forces is a common one right through history. Our modern symbol for DNA, the building blocks of life, mimics the twin twined serpents of the caduceus, the symbol of the medical community, and are taken directly from the mythology of creation.

Mythology also gives us air dragons, serpents of the sky. Azhi Dahaka may be creator of all the planets but he is also lord of the waters, a recognition of the ability of the serpent to live both above ground and below it, traveling between the worlds, yet a very chthonic creature. In fact, we think of the serpent when we think of fertility and sexuality. Carl Jung used the term chthonic, which means earthly, to mean those impulses we have that are unconscious, that rise out of the depths of our nature. In classical literature, the gods were often categorized into two camps, the Olympian (seen as gods who work from the heights, from above) and the chthonic, from the earth and the underworld below. Our Serpent archetype is a creature of the earth and our connection to it. For Jung, the snake, the serpent, has much the same impact as an archetype as the serpent had on Eve; interference in the workings of the universe will result in unconscious havoc. And we're back to Chaos. We can't really understand the serpent: cold-blooded, no appendages, "sees" with its tongue. She can shed her entire skin and immediately replace it with a new one: life and death and rebirth. Ancient cultures worshiped the snake, while the Biblical lesson is that she is to be feared, she will lead us astray, lead us to follow our unconscious longings. But on the positive side, what we don't understand about the serpent inspires in us earthly energy: creativity, passion, sexuality, our longing for immortality, those things that we know intimately only in our unconscious.

Kundalini

Widely translated as "serpent power" kundalini is an integral part in our understanding of the body from the standpoint of its energetic form. Portrayed as a serpent coiled in the first chakra at the base of the spine, the implication is that we evolve from our root upward to the top, our seventh chakra, where we unite with "spirit" or whatever we might want to call our universal connection.

Interestingly, Carl Jung wrote a seminal work on Kundalini and its symbolic representation of phases of high consciousness. Kundalini is a description of the Hero's journey to awaken his fullest potential from a base energy that resides in the spine. The Quest is salvation, in this case by uniting with the universal. Kundalini has been given a structure in the form of a yoga practice that seeks to encourage psychological and spiritual development through breath and movement.

Exercise:

In your journal note three major issues/people/things you should forgive or forget and possibly what you might do to effect the capitulation needed to let them go. Write the issues on three pieces of paper, fold them up, and put the folded papers on your Serpent altar. Don't discuss your papers or think about them further, let them be on your altar working at the level of the sacred, of myth, words are no longer necessary, no longer relevant. At some point you will notice that those papers are in your way. It might be the next day or a full moon later, but suddenly you won't even remember which paper says what, they are just in the way, just collecting dust. When this happens, without opening them again, burn them (with ceremony and intent) and dismantle your Serpent altar: you are ready for Jaguar.

Liminality

The Serpent is a daily reminder of the movement between the surface of the earth and below. She moves between worlds in a real-world way, slipping smoothly between cracks and crevices. She is a master of the Middle and Lower worlds. She is a lesson for us in holding close to the belly of the mother. At the moment when we are completely connected with all of our senses to the earth, we are able to slip below her, into the Underworld, the roots of the world tree.

Practice conscious walking: be aware of every step, who do you crush, who can follow the footsteps you have created? What chaos do you bring to the creepy crawlies? What seed scatters with your step? What flower is doomed?

If the Earth holds all of us equally, what is it that we are Giants to?

Lying quietly on the ground, stretch out your arms and embrace the grasses, the dirt, the sticks and stones. Let them inform you, let them take you beneath the earth, shift. You might even feel her rumble. Some say you might be able to ground so well in the earth that you can predict her quakes. Give it a try.

2

Jaguar

Living in the Jungle

I'm going to make the assumption here that most of us not only don't live in the jungle but have never even visited the jungle. So the question is, what is it about Jaguar that we must understand in order to pull the wisdom of the Jaguar archetype into our second chakra? Close your eyes for a moment and picture a jaguar. Imagine her padding back and forth, but please, don't put her in a cage! What does your jaguar look like? What three adjectives would you use to describe a jaguar? Fearless? Uncompromising? But compelling, right? Why are we drawn to such ferocity? I think it's partly because we want some of that. We want to have no known enemies, no foe, no fear. Right? We can get that the way jaguar does in the jungle, by being a predator, but that doesn't work in the human world as Wild Bill Hickok and Jesse James can attest or would if they hadn't been shot by someone slightly more predatory than they were.

We want to know the fearlessness of Jaguar. As shaman, we learn that the only way to know this is to meet death face to face and then step beyond death, beyond the fear of death. Have you known people who met a diagnosis of cancer with a fearless and joyful zest for life? These people are filled with the knowledge of Jaguar. The path to this fearlessness is simple: live impeccably and live right now. As we work through our twelve meditations we will talk about the Buddhist concept of karma and how that just isn't enough. Karma doesn't require enough of us, it doesn't ask us to live each breath with integrity and impeccable truth, but there is no reason we can't ask this of ourselves. We want to live in such a way that the option to live otherwise never comes up. That we never offer ourselves the choice to step outside of our core sense of certainty and integrity. Compassion and forgiveness, the positive components of "good" karma imply that there is an "I" and there is an "other" whom we have judged, or are judged by, at one time or another. In Jaguar we are stepping into an elusive idea: that we are all one when we are in balance, and to be in balance requires integrity.

For our purposes, the archetype of Jaguar resides in our second chakra. The second chakra is the seat of our sexual being. It also represents the logic part of our brain, and so we can learn to use Jaguar as an ally to "think through" basic issues. But, and this is critical, as long as we act and react from a place of Victim, we will always be the prey and not the predator. You must release the mask of Victim from your personal, karmic vocabulary. Victim tethers you to your past, of course, but even more dangerous is the fact that being a victim narrows your destiny to a predetermined tragedy that is simply not necessary. Working with the archetype of Jaguar gives you the first glimpse of a future filled with options, because you live in the immediate moment of an impeccable life. Life, not death. We will reject the Heideggerian philosophy that we are all "beings unto death" and instead think of ourselves as living the fullest life, the life of the Hummingbird, until the moment of our transition out of these human bodies in a conscious, peaceful death. To do that, the lesson of Jaguar is to embrace the fearless, impeccable certainty of Jaguar. Everything in our own private jungle is acting in concert with us, in a balanced unity, so that our enemies, if we have any, don't know we are there, and our actions are always acts of gracious integrity.

If we think about the old scare tactics of established religions, good was "us" and bad was "them" and sometimes "bad" attached itself to whole groups of people, like witches or sorcerers, or even to other established religions. The dichotomy presented is easily understood. Good versus Evil is of course a crowd management tool, such as, "We will protect you

The Death Card

In every tarot deck at position number thirteen of the Major Arcana is the card called Death. The interesting thing about this card is that contrary to the generally gruesome depictions in the card art of most decks, this card's meaning is far from negative. In fact, the Death card represents the philosophy of change, flux, transition. One deck says, "It is time to take control of your own destiny and live your life in a meaningful way…this is the time to balance the karmic books." (Golden Tarot, Kat Black). The Death card tells us that death is not an end, it is the transitive moment of every day, it is change, growth, shedding the old. Death is an invitation to renewal, reversal, regeneration. It is an opportunity. In the oldest tarot renditions, Death sometimes means literal death, but generally more often points toward the deep soul searching that signifies a complete questioning of our current way of being, Dante's "dark night of the soul." This card heralds the work that precedes the release of death (the dark) and the rebirth of life (the light). Some card readers will say we should welcome the appearance of this card as it signifies to us that we are getting nearer to our goal, shedding all that is not our true selves. The Hero's goal is transcendence of death: immortality.

from them if you obey our rules." The cultural development around this concept is deeply ingrained: in our judicial system, in our moral codes. It's very hard to get away from the good/bad dichotomy. But if we are working with Jaguar we want to work at the level where we are co-creators with the Earth and her creatures. This unification is Jaguar's mythic quest. There is no us/them, good/evil, black/white…there is only a whole earth and we upon her belly, in the moment, shed of our past, manifesting our destiny. The most important point of this is that we are self-policing. We don't need society or its religious doctrines to challenge us to "be good or else." To remain in right-balance with the earth, every word we speak must be spoken with integrity. This isn't so easy in the beginning, but you will be surprised how quickly you check yourself and swallow the negative thoughts, and then, soon enough, those mean-spirited words never even come into our heads. This is Jaguar. Of course, implicit in the requirement to be in right-balance by walking with integrity means being in a state of peace. At peace with ourselves and our differences with others, at peace with our actions to and upon the earth. In Jaguar, being true to your word is a moment by moment statement of pure integration with the earth. In order for her to survive, we must all follow Jaguar. In Jaguar there is never a moment when polluting can be forgiven, verbally or physically. Our most casual words can pollute, and that pollution will hang with us, follow us, drag us down. We must require the perfect truth of our words, of ourselves, because to do otherwise implicates us in the dualistic world of good versus evil, where recompense and forgiveness act as a sort of leveling device within which we struggle. It is too easy to use a karmic excuse, "I'm having a bad day." therefore everything I've just said can be and must be forgiven. It isn't really that hard to keep peace within oneself *and* without, and this is the state of *Grace*.

The other gift of Jaguar is the knowledge that we can turn off our high-gear, panic response to life. We are not prey. We are not being pursued. In fact, when we walk with integrity we become invisible to our enemies and our enemies fade away. Grace is what remains.

Many people experience a sense of anxiety that they cannot identify a cause for—perhaps you are walking down a crowded city street, or you are in the mall riding an escalator, and suddenly you feel aggravated or nervous, unable to concentrate on your task at hand. You're picking up energetic sludge, and that sludge has triggered your all too sensitive fight or flight reaction. Overly sensitive folks might find it useful to consciously shut down their intuitive senses before getting into their cars or going to the mall. But the next time you feel out of sorts for no reason, think about where you just were. And then take a moment to consciously shake off the sludge that belongs to someone you brushed past or stood next to, but don't send it back—they don't need it either! Brush it off with a gesture of dusting off your hands and give it all to the Earth. She loves it! She feeds on that energy and is happy to take it from you. Then consciously realign your self with your Jaguar, turn off your panic response mechanism. Next time you're in the mall with the kids you might make it through without the headache or snarky brittleness that sludge can throw at you.

Using Myths to Map the Real World

The Inka cosmology is supplying us with our first seven archetypal patterns, which we link with the seven chakras (as applied in Eastern medicine and religions), as a place to seed and hold the archetypes as sacred. The chakras serve as a focus point. It might seem odd at first to think of the sacred as belonging somewhere on our body, but it's very important to link body and soul in a way that we can see the connection as a personal map. The process by which the archetypes we each embrace allows us to shape the path that we follow in this lifetime is uniquely our own. Even though much of it affects us on an unconscious level, our real world actions are mapped by the accumulated structure of the sacred which we embrace, and which links the physical body to the spiritual by way of the chakras. While we are borrowing an Inkan map and an Eastern concept of energy centers, we fit ourselves into this structure in a way that is entirely individual, and which forms our connection to the sacred.

The sacred doesn't happen only in church on Sundays or only to the righteous. We hold the sacred within us. It's going to take some retraining to get used to the idea that the sacred is our right. It is not the provenance of a religious hierarchy. The sacred is where we do our finest and most important work as humans, and the more we can be in that framework the more direct and sweet our destiny will be. Not because we will be rewarded, but because working at the level of the sacred is the same as working within pure energy, at the level of creation. This is the true secret.

What we are looking for here when we work with myth are mechanisms by which we can bring the sacred into our literal world. Give it relevance. The archetypes and their relationship to chakras is a method by which we personalize the sacred so that we can use it as a tool for our journey. We are connecting our own singular story with the great mythological adventures so that we heal, grow and control our destiny.

The Jaguar Altar

Jaguar can become an amazing ally if you choose to work with her in depth. For many years when my son was in high school, Jaguar was my "minder." Jaguar rode in the car with him, reminded him to wear his seat belt, told him it was late and time to head home. He saw Jaguar as clearly as I did. Once, Jaguar saved his life when he went off the road and into a tree. Jaguar was there, an animal airbag.

Jaguar is also, of course, a phenomenal tracker. Develop a relationship in which you ask Jaguar to show you what you need to know, ask him to guide you. Shamans use Jaguar as their healing space guide. Open yourself to his whispers, he will show you the way.

Set your altar with new candles and items that you have collected that speak to you of Jaguar's power, and of your second chakra characteristics. Lovemaking music, exotic scent, lush fabric, jungle plants, poetry, red lipstick and gold bangles, Tibetan cats, drums, daggers, and obsidian jaguars.

Prepare your meditation space as you always do. This time perhaps you will want to work out, build up a sweat with yoga or treat your body to a sensual pleasure, paint your toes, have a full body massage. Then bathe in scented water and wrap your body loosely in a clean scented robe. You are presenting your earthly body at the altar of Jaguar. Use the sense of sight to inform your brain. Imagine you are jaguar, imagine your fur, the silence of your tread on the forest floor, the weight of your body on a strong tree limb as you suspend yourself between the worlds, waiting. Imagine your eyes as all seeing mirrors to the entire world.

When you are ready, recite the meditation. Remember to breathe, take your time with the words; they are, this time, almost a sexual encounter. Breathe and release.

The Jaguar Meditation

I am a great fire burning.
I am long, lean, sleek and powerful.
You will not know me
but I am always there, watching,
blinking, yellow eyes that see you everywhere.
Waiting.

I have no enemies in this world or the next.
I am the rainbow warrior, the peaceful one,
for I am prey to no one.
I can be called to your side,
but you must want me without condition.

I am Sekhmet, the Egyptian lioness,
my name means powerful one.
I brought the gift of fire to the Amazon.
I destroyed the Mayan First World,
consuming it for my own purpose.

I am Otorongo, Mother-Sister Jaguar,
healer, shape-shifter, shaman's familiar.
Watch the bonfire as I circle behind you,
stalk you,
I bring you your destiny,
your desire.
Look for it within the fire bright.

I am a child of the moon time,
of the early dawn
and mist filled evensong.
I am above you, and behind you,
I am your urge to love, to kill, to hunger.
Curled within you, blink and I am there,
blink and I am gone.

When your time comes
you will walk across my back to the next world
for I am Chocachinchai, the Rainbow Jaguar.
Come to me clean, open, sweetly scented.
Come to me without baggage, without cares,
come to me naked, flesh to my fur, under me
above me, my tongue will wash your past away.

Follow me, I am
the way beyond Death.

When you have finished reading the meditation, sit in stillness and experience Jaguar within yourself. Place your palms against your abdomen, cradle your second chakra as if you are receiving and cradling a cat curled up in your hands. Where and how do you feel her? What agreement would you like to make with Jaguar, how will she serve you best? As you emerge from your meditative state, bring Jaguar with you. Take a few minutes to readjust, ground yourself with food and drink and relax while you record your thoughts in your journal.

The Archetype of the Jaguar

We have learned that the practice Jaguar teaches us is to live impeccably. While Serpent challenges us to release the past, Jaguar concerns herself with our present and she offers us real and concrete tools by which to do this. For this full or new moon period, whichever you have chosen as your determinate moon cycle, learn to embody Jaguar. Learn with the sense of sight, perception. The world is as you perceive it. How then, is your world colored? Here is an opportunity for us to begin to understand Jung's concept of shadow. Jung tells us that we are duality—light and dark—and in our process to understand ourselves, we must also see that what we think is our enemy is actually a part of our self, the shadow part. That bitch at the party that always pushes your buttons only drives you crazy because she taps into the bitch in yourself, your shadow. This is such a hard concept for us to embrace, but once we can acknowledge that we all have our light and our dark aspects, we can begin to release them. The first step is to "see" that everything is perception, subjective, our own viewing of a tangled interrelated world. No one else sees through your eyes except Jaguar. Let Jaguar track your life. Jaguar looks at the "why" of your actions. When you are in your Jaguar mind you respond with "I think…" We used to think this was the greatest achievement of man, that as thinking beings we justified our superiority over the animal world. But just because you "think" it, doesn't mean anyone else will agree, right? But we are about to learn that thinking is only a lower physical state, one step toward a much higher state of being that is beyond words, beyond description, that is accessible for us within the transformative power of fine art, of music and poetry, and dance and mythology. Jaguar is the information corridor, and a valuable ally, and the voice over your shoulder when you need to adjust your focus.

The Mythology of Jaguar: Duality and Order out of Chaos

In the mythology connected with Serpent we see repeatedly that serpent's story is about creation of order from chaos. Serpent is uncontrollable, whether in water or on land. Now, in the story of Jaguar, chaos is defeated by defining worlds. It's simple: light and dark, above and below, the bad submerged beneath the earth, the good thriving in the sun above. In Aztec mythology, Tezcatlipoca is the god who ruled the sun in the first creation story. The Aztec cosmology gives five world creations, sort of five chances to get it right (we are now in the fifth). Tezcatlipoca is challenged by Quetzalcoatl, the hero of Aztec mythology and thus the figure we must learn our lessons through. We follow his journey and learn what not to do on our own. Quetzalcoatl destroyed Tezcatlipoca who transformed (shape-shifted) into a jaguar. Tezcatlipoca was known as "lord of the smoking mirror" and is often depicted with an obsidian "mirror" in his hand. He is thus being endowed with shamanic as well as godly power. He can shape-shift into his companion, Jaguar, and he can foretell the future in his "smoking mirror."

The two gods battled again and again, each time destroying worlds. As storytelling often does, later embellishments elevate Quetzalcoatl to equal status alongside Tezcatlipoca as one of four gods and brothers who created the world. Tezcatlipoca and Quetzalcoatl were known as the Black and the White. The four were the sons of the lord and lady. The duality principle is basic to the Hero's journey. Creating order, whether within our own lives or as a mythic concept is basic. At this level, our choices seem to be change or die. Black and white. Second chakra issues, procreate or die out. Dynastic. The gods of mythology learn that to successfully create a viable world, light and dark must be joined, and so, in one myth of creation, they do just that. Before they joined forces there was only water everywhere and a sea dragon (Serpent, remember her? She is the archetype Chaos) named Cipactli. The gods caught Cipactli using Tezcatlipoca's foot as bait and from the giant sea serpent's body they created land, and subjugated Chaos.

What we understand from these tales is that power through conflict causes destruction. Neither white nor black can exist on its own. Creating worlds that are successful requires bridging the dualism of above and below. Jaguar spans the worlds, he is familiar with the underworld because he works there on behalf of the shaman, and he is lord of the jungle in the Middle world. Because he moves between the worlds, Jaguar can show us the way across the rainbow bridge, the bridge between life and death, and the place of our becoming, the Upper world.

Exercise:

My teachers often use the mandala, or sand painting, as a "homework" exercise, and we almost always advise our energy medicine clients to do this work on their own after a session. If you haven't ever created a mandala before, you're in for a treat. Mandalas, labyrinths, cycle calendars, all of these visual processes are based on the magic that happens when we work within the sacred geometry of the spiral.

First, choose your medium. You can draw with colored pens on paper, you can collect stones and feathers and rocks and define a circle in the earth, you can do a traditional Tibetan circle in colored sand or use beads. You might use yarn and stones and beads, it's your choice. Define a large circle someplace where you can come back and visit the site without it being destroyed or disturbed by others.

Choose a color or a stone or other object to represent yourself and place or draw yourself into the center of your circle.

Choose a subject about your personal life that feels chaotic to you, some issue or problem that when you visit it, you get that 2nd chakra, lower gut fear response because it is out of your control. Choose one element—a stone or object or a color to represent that issue and place/draw that issue into the circle. Notice where you put it.

Choose elements to represent any people who are also involved in this issue and place them in the circle. Notice whether they land between you and the issue, inside the circle or out, are behind you or above you. Write down your thoughts as you notice these things. Don't over think the placement, just do it, and then observe the placement and look for meanings afterwards. Who has lined up with you on this matter? Who has not? Are they larger than you or smaller? How much significance have you given them.

Decorate your circle. Be creative. Tap into your child. Decorate around each of the elements, and then notice what you have created. Did some elements move? Are some covered by superficial decoration?

Leave your mandala to work without you for a while, perhaps a few days, or just overnight. Whatever feels right. What we're doing is letting the issue work itself out at the level of the myth, the level of the sacred.

When you come back to your circle, what do you notice first? Do you feel like moving some of the people elements around? Is the issue stone closer to you or is it moving off the circle completely? Sometimes you might come back and find it has disappeared! Are the people elements more aligned in a supportive structure or have they lined up against you? Is any one person positioned above you as if they have control exclusively?

Write about your impressions in your journal. You will very likely have discovered some hitherto secret aspects to the issue that now make it easier to settle and put to rest.

If your circle is made on the earth of natural elements, go back to it and destroy it by scattering all of the elements to the four directions, thanking the earth for holding your work for you. If you drew your circle, you must burn it, with honor and intention.

At the end of the month, revisit the issue you were struggling with and write in your journal how you are now able to shift your perspective, your "sight" and move forward through the jungle. Dismantle your Jaguar altar.

You are ready for Hummingbird.

3

Hummingbird

The Sweet Nectar of Life

If you're thinking "well that was easy, here I am at Hummingbird and not even half way through the book!" Think again. Yes, we're going to plant the seed of hummingbird in this meditation sequence, but this chapter is merely the bridge to the higher states of spirit to come. Hummingbird is our teacher, our guide for this journey, and so she must be resident within us now that we have prepared the ground to receive her.

I had the most trouble at this point. Hummingbird is a very difficult archetype for us Westerners to grasp, to truly embody. My first attempt to seed Hummingbird in my third chakra failed. I started off with no natural kinship for her. My observation of hummingbirds in life was that they were rather mean spirited, wee creatures who were too busy to stop and too cranky to share. In our shamanic training we are given the seed of hummingbird in full ceremonial splendor, a terrifically moving and momentous occasion. This ceremony is called the Ayni Karpi, which could almost be translated as Seeding Balance. I was anything but balanced. A few months later I was sitting at home in front of a huge window typing an e-mail to my teacher complaining that I just didn't get hummingbird at all when "Bam!" the poor thing crashed into my window, beak first. "Wow," I thought, "that wasn't very subtle."

I worked through the moon cycle struggling to incorporate hummingbird philosophy into my daily life but it wasn't until my next class, when we were able to have the seeds replanted that had not "taken" and hummingbird really did stick around, that I came to know the joy of the journey. So if this has seemed like work so far, if you are irritated that you can't wave a wand and live impeccably or leave your sad and tormented past behind, take heart. Hummingbird is on her way.

So what is it that we want to know about hummingbirds, what will inform our daily lives in such a way as to alter forever our way of approaching the dawn? Hummingbirds are amazing creatures. They have endurance, energy, and a constant thirst for the nectar of life. They are travelers, journeyers; but wherever they find themselves, they drink from the most beautiful of what the world has to offer. They are flexible, quick, and driven to survive. Their migration sometimes take them thousands of miles in its course.

What we want to remember always is this: *I drink deeply from the nectar of life.* And to do that I must be in the moment. That's the key, and for most of us, that's the rub. I want to live in the realm of what "might be." Some of us want to live in the past, where, even if we were victims, at least we knew what to expect. I want to assemble all the perfect components of a lifetime and wait for it to happen. But it will not come to us, the future never does, we have only the present. Hummingbird is going to teach you to find the sweetness in every single day and take it into your belly so that when you react you always react from a source of sweet nectar of the gods. Hummingbird is going to ask you to remember that the journey is long and requires much energy and concentration but along the way there are always opportunities for glory and for grace, options for the sacred.

Hummingbird sits in our third chakra. This chakra is our ego center and our intuition, our gut instinct. As the highest of the "lower" three chakras this level of intuition is pre-language. We don't know why, but we feel it in our gut. Later we will learn about clairvoyance, about our third eye connection to the universe as the more sophisticated, more elegant, "post-language" upper chakra kind of knowing, but this third chakra is gut instinct and it can save our lives. Always, always follow your instinct.

It's interesting that instinct and ego should be together in the third chakra, isn't it? And it makes sense. A person with a strong ego would always follow their instincts. And so if we falter in our sense of self, we lose the ability to guide ourselves. We become mothers who need how-to books in order to raise our children. We become the "dummies" all those books are aimed at. So we know that our sense of self needs to be strong, and we need to recognize that the Hero's journey is long but survivable. We need to give to ourselves first because our own healthy self esteem is the only thing that will enable us to properly give to others. Drink deeply of the nectar; it will sustain each day.

The Importance of Ritual and Ceremony

I first came to my shamanic training out of a sense of longing for community in ceremony. I come away from my training understanding that this longing is endemic. There is something within humanity that is nurtured by ritual and ceremony. When we don't find it in our daily lives, we suffer disaffection. This and this alone is enough to explain the increasing popularity of organized mega churches. But what if organized religion doesn't do it for you? What we are all longing for is ceremony that transcends the anonymous. And so we want to talk about ceremony here, in the context of the third chakra, because ritual and ceremony are the basic food for the self. What you choose to do and how you choose to do it, is not as important as this simple act of daily choosing to enact a ritual that feeds your sense of self in the wider context of connecting it to your sense of Spirit. If you suffer from isolation, jealousy, insecurity, hesitancy, or just plain fatigue, you will find healing in ceremony. Whether you ask a blessing on your food at the table, awake with praise for the dawn, stand naked in the grass to honor the moon's gentle light, it doesn't matter, as long as you do it.

Try this month to add one daily ritual to your routine. And notice the difference between those two things: ritual and routine are not the same thing! There's nothing wrong with routine, especially when it's a good habit, like exercise, but it does nothing to feed your soul and that's what we're after. When you stop to toast the Pachamama, the earth, by spilling a sip of your wine onto the ground, her belly, you recognize your responsibility to her, to this Earth that holds us all. When you make a blessing to the animals and plants that provide your dinner you know honor, you touch the sacred.

There are people who hold candle vigils, people who fast, who work in silence to a proscribed trial. There are people who say simple prayers of acceptance, calls to power, thankfulness. Become the poet and write your own simple prayer of thanks, blessing, empowerment. Create, and feel the self of your third chakra shine.

Poetry As Spiritual Practice

I used to fill blank books (or sometimes only fill a few pages of a book!) with my personal thoughts and angst ridden dreams only to discover on rereading that they needed to go into the fire, and I don't mean in a meaningful ceremonial way! I wondered how I could keep a record but not feel insecure about the life I have laid bare for others some day to read. For many years now my diary, my journaling, has taken the form of poetry writing. But it is only in the past year or two that I have found the profound value in writing poetry as a spiritual practice. If you haven't tried this, even if you have never written a poem before, this is an important way to enter into daily spiritual practice. This is how you feed your soul.

Robert McDowell's book Poetry As Spiritual Practice *(Free Press, 2008) is the perfect instructional and inspirational guide to bringing this devotional method into your life. He invites you to bring poetry out of yourself as "the pure sound and shape of spirit."*

Whether you write poetry, write prayers, journal compulsively or only erratically, elevating the method by which you set down your thoughts on a daily basis to the level of the sacred is one more way to achieve ritual and ceremony in your life. And it's one of the best ways.

The Hummingbird Altar

There are specific things for your altar: maps for the journey; these might be literal maps, or they might be photographs of important events. We are mapping the soul here as well as the literal world. Your map might be encoded in poetry, I can think of the poet Mary Oliver as a map maker here. Nectar: honey, of course, and flowers, what are your favorites? Study the stamens, the petals, the leaves, the stems. If you don't already work with flower essences, this is the time to learn about the energetic power of flowers. Hummingbirds know. Compose your altar of things you will need for your journey, your figurative or literal maps and compass instruments.

Preparing for this meditation means spending time out of doors watching nature. Watch the jasmine open at night. What attracts the hummingbirds in your garden? Watch their flight pattern as they fly up to their nests. Did you know that different kinds of hummingbirds fly in different arcs? Sit quietly in the grass and soak up the juicy, luscious colors around you. Bathe naked in a pool or clear stream. Put flowers in your hair to attract hummingbird. Then lie quietly on your back, your hands open, palms up. You are available, ready for the sky and beyond, ready for the journey. Breathe in joy.

The Hummingbird Meditation

Sira Q'inti, Hummingbird!
On the silver spirit wings of grandmothers
I fly.
I am a thousand beats of heart and wing.
I am one song
one sweetness.
Taste the nectar,
for the journey is long.

I am Colibris, Bird of the Sun.
I am unstoppable
uncatchable
iridescent and soaring.
I bring you the ancestors
for they are my familiars
their journey has no end,
call to me and you call to them.

I am fearless, indefatigable
and I am your defender.
I am long life and I know no hardship.
I am the secret whisperer
drops of nectar on your lips,
I am the guardian of your destiny.
Follow me, the path is long
and it is sacred.
I hold the future and I hold the past.

I know the key:
Drink deeply of the nectar of each day.
Even sustenance, even simple survival is sweet.
I am rebirth, I am hope.

I am your guide, follow me,
we will celebrate together.
I am the pure energy of your heart.

I am your guide,
I am the master of time,
with me everything,
everything becomes sacred,
follow me.
I am Hummingbird.

The Mythology of Hummingbird

From Hummingbird my teacher says we learn to "drink directly from the knowledge of the mountain." This is the mythic life journey. We have our first taste of the sacred at the energetic level of action where thought and language are already and have never been. Hummingbird is a state of knowing. What we know is the connection to universal truths, to the mountain.

Hummingbird is a New World animal, so the myths and legends about hummingbird are limited and generally restricted to South America. In Peru, there are more than a hundred different kinds of hummingbirds. There are Quechua love songs about hummingbird, and she has many names in their language: Colibris, Picaflores, Q'inti; they are birds of the sun.

A Quechua myth tells of a time when the world was barren and dry; everyone was dying because it did not rain. A tiny hummingbird struggled to take flight, rising off of the last flower alive and she flew up to the god Waitapalana and begged him to save the land, and she wore herself out so much with her trial that she then died. Waitapalana shed two crystal tears in sadness at the hummingbird's death, and when they fell from the god's eyes they landed on the Serpent, Amaru, who was sleeping at the bottom of a lake. The serpent awoke with a start and stretched and shook his wings, and from his wings water fell as rain and the world was saved.

For some Northwest Coast Native tribes of North America, Hummingbird symbolizes good fortune and good weather, and sometimes hummingbirds are said to attract love. Most mythology involves an arduous journey for hummingbird who catches rides on the backs of geese, or shape-shifts as a part of a longer Hero's quest. Often the quest involves water, definitely the element associated with this thirsty bird. Both the Hopi and Zuni cultures have myths involving Hummingbird convincing the gods to bring rain.

For some cultures, Hummingbirds represent our dead ancestors, and so in our prayer to open sacred space we shaman call "Hummingbird, Grandmothers, Grandfathers!" Hummingbirds are the renewer of life, the sacred pollinator.

Hummingbird is changeable and there are many legends in which the light shining on hummingbird's feathers is an important lesson about when we "shine" and when we are plain and dull, the elusive quality of beauty and perception. In a beautiful Mayan legend, Hummingbird disguises himself as the Sun in order to make love to a beautiful woman who is actually the Moon. Hummingbird reminds us always to adapt, work within the journey, be in control of the moment, and stay awake to the potential of the gifts each day offers. Not every day holds greatness, not every day offers us opportunity to shine our colors the brightest, but each day does offer something, some sweet moment. The journey is long so that we may enjoy every part of it.

Exercise:

When I was first learning to meditate I discovered Jack Kornfield, the American Buddhist, and his lovely and inspiring books about learning to meditate the Buddhist way. For years I would drive down the crowded highway near San Francisco repeating:

"Compassion, compassion, compassion…." Now, when I'm driving, I hear that in my head all the time!

In your journal, write a simple salutation that you can remember and repeat each morning to remind you to taste the sweetness of the day. Craft it so that it is short and clear and easy to recall. Find a turquoise stone and put it next to your bed, near the clock, so that when you wake in the morning it is the first thing you will see. That stone represents the sun, the joy of a new day, and it will remind you to say your salutation. The use of a piece of turquoise as the first thing you look at is a Native American tradition.

Shape-Shifting

Most shaman, no matter what their cultural background, are attributed the skill of shape-shifting. The ability to slip between the sensory worlds adopting the shape and manner of an animal "familiar" is cultivated within the meditation process. It requires a deep relationship with the animal, a very real ability to "get inside the animal's skin." Shaman use shape-shifting in their healing work, in effecting protection, and in the divination techniques that they use.

My teacher tells about a time during his early training where a shaman elder followed him around in the guise of a condor. His own teacher could see the great bird of prey stalking him. (To read more of this exciting story see Dance of the Four Winds, *by Alberto Villoldo.) I can assume the shape of an owl. Working between the realms of reality in this way often serves the additional purpose of removing us from earthly attachments while we do our meditation work. It's a level of freedom. We use shape-shifting as a way of being when the work to be done cannot be done effectively in our own bodies.*

Shape-shifting requires a highly skilled degree of sustained meditation. It also requires a natural affinity for the creature you assume. Who is your kin in the animal world?

4

Eagle

The Soaring Heart

I'm such a romantic. I get to this chakra, the Heart chakra, and all I can do is just give a big sigh. You know? But there's more to the Heart chakra, the fourth chakra, than love. There is a fierceness and tenacity in a strong heart chakra that we haven't seen in the lower three chakras because they are in so many ways less evolved. In our fourth, we become complicated. ("Oh boy, do we ever" you're saying, especially you guys.) What do we have in the heart chakra that is so different? We have the moment in our journey toward achieving the level of the sacred when we turn our attention outward for the first time. We do have vulnerability in matters of the heart in our weaker aspect, it's true, but in our strongly manifest aspects, we have that fierce quality that makes mothers towering giants of power in defense of their children, that made Romeo take poison rather than live without his Juliet, that made Joan of Arc give her life for a cause she recognized as greater than her own life. The fierce defense of the heart is Eagle.

Think of the Eagle at perch, imagine him on a stark tree branch, giant wings folded in the warming sun, head tucked, eyes bright and open. The shape of Eagle in this pose is that of a heart. Do you see it? Eagle is the archetype that takes the love and loving grace of the heart and brings it to the universe as patriotism, as global awareness, as generosity. Without the important moment of stepping into Eagle we would not care for our fellow man. I've always noticed that Aquarians seem to be in Eagle more than the rest of us. They fight our causes in the global arena passionately and at the expense of their personal lives. But we all need, particularly now, to step into Eagle and soar.

The fourth chakra, matters of the heart. We aspire to Eagle, but often we suffer some pretty vividly described crises in this chakra. Broken hearted. I'm not even sure Cupid's image of a heart with an arrow piercing through it is such a good idea. Who needs to start out in love with a hole in his heart? When we align this chakra with the Hero's journey we see that the Hero in us opens to interacting with the world from the perspective of passion. In the Hero's tale, he always meets at least one woman he falls in love with. And often this woman represents either something he must fight for ("man-up"), or she is leading him astray, off his path, away from his destiny. Why does the Hero have to meet this challenge in the heart chakra before he is allowed to know the sweetness of love? Well, I guess it's for the sake of the morality tale, but it does seem to be that way in life too, doesn't it? It is when we give our heart away that we learn our biggest lessons. Only a few of us are fortunate enough to go through life without a broken heart at one time or another. But the Hero in the Grail Quest has finally discovered that he can't make the journey alone, he can't move forward based on the lower three chakras. We all know people who are trying to do just that, but it doesn't work. Everyone needs love, needs passion, needs to interact with the global community. If we can enter the realm of Eagle, we gain perspective, perspective over the whole world and our place in it. Our shaman prayer for Eagle says, "let me fly wing to wing with Great Spirit." We're asking for objectivity so that we can make the Hero's decisions and move along the path toward our greatest destiny. And we're asking for it from the heart, the most subjective and vulnerable place on our body. This is what makes us human and complicated. We're asking ourselves to step into Eagle, to see the world from above, from the high ground, but to do it from the heart. If we all did this, globally, think what a different world we could create. Fierce love, instead of "tough love."

Shamanically, Eagle brings us light, comes to us from the place of the rising sun, the East direction, the Upper world, as opposed to Serpent who dwells beneath the earth and never moves in a straight line. Eagle is straightening out his path, linking his destiny to the sacred. My teachers say, "Eagle will show us the mountains of our dreaming." In Eagle and from the heart chakra we choose our destiny, make wishes into reality, strive for our higher purpose. The color associated with the heart chakra is silver, for the feminine, for the Moon as well, for the strides we can make even in our dreaming.

In Eagle we let matters of the heart guide our self. Though we all hope we do this gracefully, often we fail and fall crashing to the earth. Remember the myth of the boy who made wings from wax and flew too close to the sun? His aspirations were set too high, the gods thought him cheeky and impertinent. The gods thought he wanted to be a god! We want to take chances with our heart, but not mortally. No one ever died of a broken heart. The effort of flight is part of the destiny, part of the learning process.

But, let's not forget Hummingbird in all of this big, predatory, bird talk. Now that we have Hummingbird firmly installed, we have thrown out a line to our destiny. Eagle will show us the big picture. Eagle will draw the global map, and on the map will be challenges and corrections, sadness and joy, but it will be your journey, embrace it! Become Hummingbird! When you have questions about the quest you are on, ask Eagle to fly high with you, give you perspective sight. Eagle will show you how you fit in to the grand plan. Eagle will show you the path to the sacred.

The Eagle Altar

Spend some time out doors where you can observe birds in the sky, particularly raptors if you have that wonderful opportunity. The predatory birds spend a lot of time very, very high in the sky, circling in arcs. I have seen turkey vultures flying in gangs, arcing circles around and around, searching for the dead. I've seen them waking from their morning perch, six, seven or more birds gradually unfolding their great wings to dry in the morning sun, as if the trees' black branches have suddenly come alive. Eagles take partners, nest high, high up. They fly high, soaring, watching. They see so much more of the earth than we do. Observe this about the larger birds.

On your altar, place a heart shaped stone. Around the stone, create your greater world in microcosm using symbolic tokens—stones, feathers, leaves, perhaps a ribbon as your destiny line. You'll know what needs to be there. What represents the destiny line you are creating? What is stalking you? What are the obstacles? Money can't buy you love, but if it's lack of money that keeps you in a dead-end job or prevents you from getting an education that will open your world, then put a coin someplace on your altar. This altar is like your mandala work. For the month, you will be reworking the arrangement of obstacles and the destiny line and your heart, so take your time choosing the tokens and images you will use.

Before you begin, prepare your body. Spend some time in the sun, warm your wings. Observe the methods you used to construct your altar, notice the obstacles, what is stalking you? Just put these formative questions into the back of your consciousness so that they can do their work while you are in a meditative state. Now you are in Eagle; you don't have to do all of your work in the conscious world of the spoken word. We don't need story now, we can work our own process by giving up our story to the great myths and in so doing we map a sacred path in the energetic world where language does not exist. Imagine it as if the chosen destiny of each of us is a star thrown out into the night sky. Now we want to let the stars inform us without language. Let them inform us by their mere being, by the energetic thread that connects each of us to our destiny star, so that when we stand outside on a clear night, we are drawn to one particular star and feel the tug of energy as we connect with it.

Light a candle. If possible sit in a way that when your eyes are open you are looking directly down at your altar from above. When you complete the meditation itself, Open your eyes gently and assess your altar arrangement, analyze it, enjoy it, let it inform you. Breathe.

The Eagle Meditation

I am Apuchin! Great Eagle, Condor,
I am lord of thunder,
I carry a lightning bolt in my talon.
I have no enemies in the sky,
I am above the rest, I see all.

I am Horus, the falcon-headed god,
I am the Norse God, Wodan, and
Roman Mercury. Zeus am I.
My rune stands for the gift of ecstasy.
I have the power to bind
and to loose.

I am power and fierce presence,
thunder is the beating of my wings.
I am one of the Evangelists,
Angels seek me out.
I am the solar heat of the sun
and I am the sky god.

I am inspiration and strength
I am the element of Air
and I come from the East.
I am the triumph of spirit,
when you work through me
you work through god.

I am Eagle, Spirit flight, Wakiyan, helper god,
Thunderbird, lord of the mountain,
Hino, Thunder Spirit, guardian of the sky,
Hatun Apuchin, Great Eagle.
I come to teach you to fly with Great Spirit.
Reach with me for the mountains of your dreaming,
I will take you there.

Altar Work

As you opened your eyes from your Eagle meditation, what did you notice first about your altar? Spend some time now with your altar. Use the softened gaze of the meditation state to *alter* your perception. When you soften your gaze, that sort of dazed looking but not looking we all do when we're tired, what do you see? Is the stone that represents your heart prominent? Has it disappeared? Is it in the center, truly, of the activity around it? Or is it covered by some obstacle? Has it shifted? Does it seem overpowered? How does it lie in conjunction with your destiny line object? If you have one, take a feather and in a clockwise motion twirl the air above your altar with the feather. What moved? What shifted? What do you see now? Write down your impressions in your journal.

Stepping into Eagle is stepping onto the path of the sacred. Here we learn the gift of intention, and intention leads to manifestation. At the level of the sacred, everything is possible. Your task is to decide what your sacred destiny is, and plant that seed in your heart chakra. Allow Eagle to show you the possible, allow your heart to give you the probable, and then follow Hummingbird, for he knows the way for you.

As always, when you conclude your meditation session ground yourself with "cakes and ale" as the witches say, meaning have a little something to eat, drink some water, dance, shake your body out. Breathe. Probably best not to drive a car immediately after meditating, and certainly don't try to fly!

The Mythology of Eagle

Eagle is so often identified with thunder in mythology. In Greek myth Zeus used Eagle as his shape-shifting animal so that he could control thunder and lightning. In several Greek myths Zeus changes into Eagle in order to satisfy his lust, once for Ganymede, a beautiful young boy, and again for the kidnapped girl Europa. In another tale, Zeus set two eagles on the task of circling the earth, one from one direction, one from another; wherever they would meet, that would be the center of the world. They met, according to the tale, in Delphi, and there Zeus placed a stone called an "omphalos" and set a serpent to guard it, and

Synchronicity

Synchronicity is when the sacred and our destiny meet. This is why inventions are often "invented" by several people, or cultures, at the same time even though they have never had contact with each other. Take weaving, for example. At some point, many thousands of years ago, a talented woman in Mongolia got tired of making cord and stringing nuts on it and decided instead to figure out a way to twine cord into a flat fabric. She did it in a very simple way at first, but gradually, because it was her destiny to be creative in this way, she invented a loom. And then she went looking for softer fibers and a way to make them into cord and invented spinning linen and cotton. But at the same time, there was a man in Africa, impossibly far removed from Peru or Mongolia, who did the same thing, for the same destiny and from the base of the same gifts. And this is how weaving on looms came about in many different areas of the world at nearly the same time in terms of human development. They just happen because the timing demands it, because the universe is ready.

Some things are just ready to be. This is synchronicity. What is it about the destiny you dream that resonates with your friends? That makes them say, Yes! Me too! I want that! What is it about your dreams that you might bring to all of us as a sacred gift? Look for the synchronous patterns in your life, and you will find the path of the sacred.

an oracular priestess lived in the sanctuary, and her predictions were known to always come true.

In ancient Hittite and Sumerian myths from the Near East, Eagle is the supreme god and often identified with Serpent, the god of above battling with the god of below. In Zu we have already seen Eagle and Serpent combined as a winged Serpent/dragon. In one Mesopotamian culture the Eagle was two-headed so that it could see all and never be surprised.

The identification with snakes is common wherever eagles are found. Mexico City stands where it does today because of a myth in which the Aztec god told his people to find the place where the eagle sits on a cactus and eats a snake and make that their home.

In some Native America traditions, shaman use Eagle feathers to cleanse the aura and to facilitate shape-shifting. The thunderbird is one of the most powerful and predominant of Plains Indians images. For the Northwest Coast Bella Coola the creator ancestor came down to earth as an Eagle. The Thunderbird for the Haida represented the ultimate shape-shifter, and a time when there was no difference between animal and human.

The Thunderbird is the godlike manifestation of Eagle. In the beating of his wings we hear the thunder, the blink of his eyes, lightning. Thunderbird comes on earth to fight the forces of evil, often represented as Serpent, thus creating violent weather and earthquakes. To have a personal relationship with Thunderbird is a powerful life altering experience. To have been struck by Thunderbird's lightning is seen as a sign of great spiritual power and many shaman are known to have been struck by lightning and survived, transformed by the call to power.

In early Christianity the Eagle symbolized the resurrection, thus Eagle is a symbol of creation. Eagle is a gateway archetype, breaching the heights of the Middle world to give us psychic and spiritual access to the wisdom of the ancients. This mystical pathfinder quality is nearly universal. Spirituality, mysticism, thunderous power; Eagle is an archetype of the higher realm.

In Norse mythology, the god Wodan carries Eagle as his symbol, and Eagle again is connected with divination, the sky, and power. Wodan had the power to bind which he used on the battle field to hamper his enemies. The Norse divination tool, rune stones, has a rune of Wodan. Wodan is often credited with having created the rune divination devices and his stone represents joy, creative fire, aspirations. We see the Norse god Wodan usually representing the Earth element but also transiting between earth and sky in his role as creator, giver of joy. The rune Wodan challenges us to set lofty goals and suggests that our wishes are attainable. Reach for the sky the way Eagle does.

The Norse Eagle sits at the top of the world tree, Yggdrasil, and Serpent lies beneath the earth at the base of the tree, twined around the tree's roots, but there is communication between them. A squirrel runs between the top and bottom of the world, transferring information, keeping the Upper world and Lower world connected and on track. Wodan (also known by the translation Odin) shape-shifted between Eagle and Serpent. In one story, Odin, as Serpent, lies with the daughter of a giant for three nights in order to seduce her into sharing the magic mead of inspiration. As soon as he has drunk completely of the mead, the serpent Odin changes into Eagle and flies off with the magic liquor in his beak. Odin, the Eagle, returns to the gods and spits the liquid into their cups. And so from Eagle we get joy, but not simple joy, the joy of creative inspiration.

Another battle between Odin and the Giants involved the quest for immortality. In this story it is the Giant who changes form into an Eagle. There is the usual kidnap of a vulnerable woman that always seems to occur in myths (representing fertility, source of life as power) and lots of shape-shifting all around. What becomes apparent in these Norse myths is that Eagle is power and represents the masculine. Many Norse myths tell of women in bird form, but they are never predators, they are often carrion eaters, scavengers. What does this say about the archetype of Eagle? He comes from the sun, meaning the Light or good source, he is masculine energy of creation, power, and cunning. When we have Eagle, we get what we want. Eagle transcends the earth and takes our aspirations to the level of the sacred, pure creative force. A friend of mine was put off by the notion of Eagle as good masculine energy because she thinks of Eagle as co-opted by the United States and as such she doesn't want to identify with that warlike aggressive behavior. For our purposes, we want to embrace the Eagle's power of the sun, go back to the source archetype: the creative power of dreaming big that masculine energy can bring to us.

Exercise:

This is the most important exercise in the book. Take your time. This isn't about fame and fortune, love life, or jobs. It's time to begin "dreaming your world into being." It's time to "grow corn," as my teachers would say.

Synchronicity:

Begin from Eagle – from your dreams, from the long view. In your journal write about the synchronicity in your life. What events have occurred that have set you on this course of discovery? Who did you meet, what book did you read, who were you talking with over a glass of wine when the bell rang or the light went on and you got excited. There is no such thing as a fast way to a pile of money in the bank. It's not important. What is important is to have a full and fierce heart that is working for a dream, a destiny. This is working at the level of the Sacred.

Generosity:

Next, make a list of the five things you feel most passionate about. Then reorder them such that those that are most accessible to you, that will be most easily put into effect, are at the top of your list. Pick the one that makes your heart swell with excitement, with joy, with pride, with compassion and list three ways you could become involved. Which of those three is the most likely to succeed? Put it on your calendar. This is your starting point.

Grace:

Oddly enough, dreams, destiny, synchronicity, these elements don't come from an "I." They don't come from the self, they aren't about us. They are universal tetherings that bring us in line with the sacred. They create Grace. The passion you have chosen to start out with on your journey as Hummingbird might not be the final, ecstatic dream of this lifetime for you, but it is a start, and it is where you must begin; because to walk the path of the sacred journey, you have to give.

Make a plan. Check in with Eagle periodically if you need to adjust your perspective. Work your altar, remove obstacles, recognize pathways, blow creative fire across your working. Never let a day begin without checking in with your altar. Begin the journey.

Cosmology

What comprises the ancients' idea of universe? We're beginning, as we look into the mythical world view, to see patterns. The universe contains three parts, envisioned as the Great World Tree. The Lower world, the Underworld, is beneath the earth's crust. For some it is the land of the dead, but not for all. Sometimes it is the realm of Chaos, of unstructured, unrestrained beginning, ruled by Serpent. The Middle world is where we live in human form, the "real" world of tangible, mortal life. The Middle world is where we act out our Hummingbird's journey informed by the Lower world and the Upper world. The Upper world is the land of spirit, the unknowable that we all have known and will know again. Knowledge comes from its purest form in this realm. The Upper world includes the stars, the sun and moon, ancient galaxies that hold our ancestors, and galaxies whose time has yet to come that will inform our children.

How the worlds came to be and in what way they interact is cosmology. The creation stories, the "first story" are the telling of a world philosophy in myth form, as a tale that always begins "Once upon a time." What story can you tell?

5

The Lower World God

As Above, So Below

When we think and act at the level of the cosmos, the universe as a whole, and ourselves fluid within that whole, we begin to walk between the worlds and expand the limits of our five basic senses. We want to think of the worlds, Upper, Middle and Lower, as rooms within the house that is our Universe. We sometimes think of these worlds in terms of the structure of our own consciousness, thus "Upper world" becomes the super-conscious, "Middle world" becomes our conscious mind, and "Lower world" becomes the subconscious. The five senses we all use are active within the Middle world, the world of our waking everyday reality; but we have other active senses that allow us access to the deep pathways of our own unconscious workings and that connect us to the universe as well. We all have the ability to develop the skills needed to explore these other worlds, to master our other available senses. The Upper and Lower world act as mirrors, reflecting the sacred parts of the universe back onto the Middle, back to us.

In our archetypal journey as Hummingbird we visit these worlds in order to access our additional senses. We visit them to engage with guides who will give us a taste of the expansiveness of the universe, and enliven and enlarge our opportunities so that we may follow the path of our most creative destiny. If we stay locked in the literality of the Middle world at the level of only our basic five senses, we cut ourselves off from a great ocean of potential. Whether we are sitting in the garden in the literal world asking the lily to share her medicine with us, or journeying to the star nations to seek our guiding star, as Hummingbird and Hero we will drink from the nectar as we find it and seek the path that is our finest at every turn.

In our sleep we use the most easily accessible of these extra senses: the knowledge that comes to us in our dreaming. In our dreaming state we are able to connect to the Upper and Lower worlds and bring information from these realms into our waking state by way of our remembered dreams. The next step is to actively participate in the dream. We've all done that. It's the moment when you are just about to wake up but you don't want to leave the dream where you're about to kiss the cute guy, so you actively try to stay asleep. Or you're in the middle of a nightmare, the snake is just about to bite and you want out of that dream immediately! Researchers call this "lucid dreaming" and it can be a powerful divinatory tool. Working between the worlds, whether the Lower world or the Upper world, is like lucid dreaming. We are actively seeking to step into a highly colored and complex sequence of images that show us the parts of the universe that lie beyond that of ordinary reality. It takes guidance and careful intention to navigate these other worlds. The Archetypes of the next three chakras are our guides for this work.

Working in the Lower world asks us to allow ourselves to dive deeply into the earth in order to connect with the past and the possible. As a means to navigate within the "room" that is the Lower world we ask for a guide, and this guide we will call a god or lord in the traditional pagan way because mythology is a powerful trigger for opening the often locked doors of this non-standard realm. We will see that this figure, just like the animal archetypes we have met in the first four meditations, takes many faces and forms and might have a completely different and new aspect for you personally. Do not be put off by the designation of god or lord, but see it as a title of reverence for a mighty and powerful force, a force that lies within you and is yours to call.

The Lower world archetype lies in the fifth chakra, the lowest physical point of the upper three chakras (the fifth chakra being the throat area, the sixth chakra is the third eye positioned at your forehead, and the seventh is at the crown of your head). The fifth chakra is your area of communication. I've observed that often people who are not allowed to speak their minds will use their hands to rub their throats or muffle their throat area with scarves and shawls tamping down the needs of their fifth chakra. See if you notice this yourself. Someone speaking to you and searching for the right word or phrase will pull at their throat as if physically trying to extricate the language of the soul. When we dig deep for the language that will best express our truest selves, we access the knowledge of our personal guides from beyond the literal world.

The three world archetypes are difficult areas to access for the first time. You may find yourself struggling with one area in particular, while another world is easy for you to slip into. The one you can access without difficulty is the one you have already been working in without knowing you were doing so. We all do this in our dream work. For me, it's the Lower world.

When I started my training with The Four Winds Society, the dean of the program was teaching how to check whether the seeded archetypes had "taken" root in our chakras and she asked for a volunteer. Since I suspected that my hummingbird archetype had not taken, I raised my hand and since I never raised my hand in class I think she was surprised and happy to have a chance to work with me. When she got to the point in the demonstration where she tested my fifth chakra she laughed, "Oh! You spend a lot of time down there don't you?" And it was true. For many years I had been in the habit of visiting the Lower world, particularly during the time of Samhain, or the Day of the Dead, when traditionally the veil between the worlds is at its thinnest and access is much easier. The process by which I journeyed to the Lower world on my own varied only slightly in minor details from that which we learned in our shamanic training. The meditation journey for accessing these worlds should be seen as a device.

One person's description of the "road" might not match your own, but that doesn't mean you aren't doing it right; above all else, accept what you see. Don't try to manage the images that come before you. Acknowledge them and accept them as valid. This is the hazard in all guided meditation. Beware of the notion that your path has to be exactly like your teacher's, and don't be distracted by a guided meditation that isn't giving you a mirror to your own journey. This is why we use archetypes to bring us out of our own thinking selves (and out of anyone else's portrayal as well) and into the mythic. Remember the definition of mythic? It's a description of a story told. It's not the literal facts, but it's the story everyone gets because we have all told the story ourselves for many lifetimes. The mythic is in our DNA. In this meditation's homework exercise you will be asked to work your own second meditation journey to identify the pathway to the Lower world that works for you.

Like all good Hero's tales, we are now asking ourselves to travel beyond the realm of the earthly world in order to gain insight into our destiny. Traditionally, this journey to the Lower world contains an element of danger. And you will experience that sense of threat if you view the dead and their domain as something awful to be feared. So let's try to dispel these rather modern concepts of "hell and damnation" and dreadful ghostly threats, which are quite new in terms of human cosmology, and that come to us implicit in the dichotomy required by Western religion: that for there to be good, there must be evil, and where better for evil to reside but deep beneath the earth, with the dead, in Hell. Instead, let's look at what really lies beneath the earth: the base from which all life springs, right? Where do we plant? Where are the core elements of life? We want to see these other territories of the universe as accessible realms where the spirits, ancestors, angels, guides—the master catalog, if you will, of all creation, past and future—reside.

And so our Hero's quest is about to take us to the Lower world in search of allies. The lord of the Lower World, for the Q'ero, is called Huascar and is so named for the Inka king who was banished to the Lower world. Huascar means Gentle Hummingbird. The Q'ero see him as masculine. In Celtic lore we match Huascar with The Green Man, who is himself a representation of the fertility of the earth, and so he wears a crown of leaves and sometimes rather resembles an old tree himself. But there are also feminine representations of the Lower world god/goddess. My favorite is the Lady of the Lake. Myth from the British Isles almost always involves water. Here we find that access to the Lower world comes from crossing a lake to a misty island inhabited by the wisest of women. Even the power of the sword comes to man only by the grace of the water and her power. Remember the myth in which the sword is thrown into the lake only to rise again with the right and true king?

One particularly effective meditation is the journey over or through water. When I was first learning to meditate I imagined myself a sea otter wrapped in kelp. I still use that image if I am trying to meditate in a particularly distracting setting—onboard an airplane or in a classroom.

In order for us to make our Hero's quest we need guides. Without them we would have to reinvent the wheel every time we encountered a challenge. This way, with the Archetypes to assist us, we can move smoothly toward realizing what our destiny is and how to achieve it without using up this entire lifetime in the process.

In your work in the worlds you will be challenged to find your own guides. Pay particular attention to him or her. How is he dressed? Who accompanies her? What is her name? Also be aware that you might be challenged by a spirit who pretends to be what he is not, and so you must always ask, "Who are you?" We offer you the archetype in many forms within the meditation poem itself. Your work is to make the journey your own.

The Lower World Altar

Your altar is a personal representation of the connection you have to this archetype. The Lower world is the realm of the dead, of animal spirits, and of spirit guides, and as such it is populated and guarded by the people who were forced underground into the dark and away from the light. In Celtic mythology, the light was represented by the race called the Tuatha dé Danann. The race that preceded them were the Firbolgs, little people who were forced underground through the liminal spaces such as caves, lakes and rivers. The mythology of these ancient times survives for us in Halloween. While for most of the year our literal world has strong barriers against the liminal so that we do not easily travel between the worlds, for some reason during Halloween the veil becomes thin, becomes an opportunity for us to move easily between the worlds, and for spirits to move between them as well. If you have trouble journeying between the worlds in your early meditations, try it on Halloween. For the Celts, Halloween is New Year's Eve. It is the beginning of the dark period of winter, the period of the dead. It is a time for storytelling, for remembering and honoring the ancestors. It is a time to come to the fire and sit with your clan, alive and dead, and invest yourself in the lineage that you can call your source.

Totem Animals

We can call on many different kinds of guides in our journey from Fool to Enlightened Hero—angels, spirits, gods, ancestors, fairies. One of the most useful and most common guides is a totem animal. Sometimes we have one loyal companion who has been with us since we were infants and we knew the language of animals before we knew how to speak. Sometimes we have an animal guide who is only with us for a day, or a single event, or appears just to give us a clue as to this particular moment of our journey. We can find these totem animals in two ways: the first is for the animal to appear to us in the literal world—an owl flies in front of your car, a sea otter follows your kayak. The second is to journey to the Lower world to ask for a totem animal to work with you. Once you are comfortable with your Lower world meditation skills, make a journey to meet your totem animal. When you arrive, Huascar will assist you, since among other things he is Lord of the Animals. Many animals will come to greet you, but only one will connect with you. Ask if the animal will work with you, talk with it about what you want from your relationship. Ask it to return with you to the Middle, literal world. Thank Huascar for keeping you safe while you connected with your new animal and make the return journey bringing your animal with you. There are many books available on interpreting animals and the messages the animals bring to us that are sometimes quite astonishing. Do some research about your animal so that you know its habits and symbols.

If you already work with guides, include them in the composition of this altar. In assembling your altar remember the path to the Lower world. It is the roots and deep earth, the kelp bed and the ocean floor and beyond. It is fecund, alive, warm, dark and wet. Your candles might be black, the incense a natural plant and heavy in scent. You will work in a completely darkened space. Make a pathway with tea light candles to a center circle where your altar is built. When you are ready, enter the room now lit only with candles. As you follow your path to the center, blow out each tea light candle until you are in the middle of the darkened room with only your altar before you for light. This is your earth womb path, your threshold. Breathe.

The Huascar Meditation

Come to me.
Where is your portal?
Settle beneath an ancient gnarled oak,
a towering snowcap mountain.
Settle in the silence beneath the rain forest canopy,
deep in the sway of ocean wave,
or under the heating bath of desert sun.
Become the earth.
Choose your portal, but come to me.
I am Huascar Inka, Lord of the world below,
Keeper of the Dead,
I am "the one who brings together."

Descend:
through peat dark earth, thick and clotted,
be guided by the greatest and longest of the roots
and vines surrounding you,
the swaying strands of kelp in the murky sea,
or caverns deep and slick,
for I am everywhere below,
waiting for you.
Come.

Descend:
Feel your precious body reshape and fit as you
slip into the mother's core—
mere breath of energy within the expanse of the
heart of her.
I am Lord of the Lower World.
Seek me out.
A doorway, a cave, a flowing river may have brought you this far—
Find your feet, your hands, your heart:
Bring your whole self to this moment.

Come:
Through the doorway, the cave opening,
the slip of time and space between tall stones:
Where are you? What do you see?
A beautiful wild forest grove full with animals,
sprites, people of the otherworld,
ancestors, and more.
Be there...seek me out.

Make your bow, your honoring, I am Huascar,
my name means Gentle Hummingbird,
I am Lord and more.
I am known by many names,
I have many faces and can shift my shape as I please
and you may know me as you wish.

To you I may have a female guise,
ancient and weathered or young and lithe.
To you I may be the Lady of the Lake, or
Persephone, goddess of the budding grain,
known as Kore to some, caretaker of the creatures of the Earth.
I reflect the seasons of your journey: I may be
Maiden, Mother or Crone, Calaich, Witch, or Virgin.
I am Queen. Hecate can be my name.

To you I may be Lord, the Green Man am I.
Cernunous the Horned God, Lord of the Animals
or Osiris the Egyptian God.
I am known as Arawan the Welsh God of Terror,
War, and Revenge.
And I am the Irish God, Labraid, and I am King of
the Faeries, called Mider.
I am Herne the hunter, Lord of the Hunt,

and I am Aericura, the Under World god of gods.
I am the Hindu, Pasupati, surrounded by beasts of many colors.
I am Hades, the Innkeeper, Persephone
I took by force as my wife.
And I am known as Pluto.
I am the Shape-Shifter, know me by my many faces.
Look around you. Who do you see?
I am Huascar, Lord of the Animals.
Make your bow before me
but know also that I am your ally, your teacher, your guide.
You will come to me to seek your animal guardians.
I will introduce you
to the people of the Lower world, the ancestors,
and you will walk at my side among them.
I am the grantor of access to secrets of many lifetimes.
You will pass this way often on your quest:
for truth, for shadow,
for your own soul's reparation.

I am Huascar, the Inka.
Besieged by the Conquistadors,
betrayed by my brother.
Murdered and banished below forever.
Like the Serpent,
I slither beneath the surface of the earth and here I reside,
Serpent in her highest form.
Come to me.

Come to me for truth and courage.
I am the peaceful one,
and I am the magnificent warrior.
The dead are my companions,
the spirits are my guides.

Come to me and we will explore your shadow,
your allies, your ancestors.
Who are the Dead who gather 'round at your seeking?

I am the Gatekeeper. Lord of Life and Death.
I am Huascar.
I am Lord of all animals,
keeper of the chambers of your soul.

I am Huascar and I reside in you.
Touch your throat in prayer pose:
Breathe…me…
now.

Core Lower World Meditation Path

Many great shamanic teachers have gathered diverse practices from around the world and formed them into what are known as "core" values or teachings. They do this so that those of us without an indigenous lineage can learn some of the most valuable systems used in energy medicine. One such core practice is the Lower World journey. Stripped of its archetypal embellishments, this journey is basic and a perfect beginning process to learn and use on your own. This is an entry meditation, to be combined with specific purposes or agenda such as soul retrieval, but this is the starting point work.

Close your eyes. Imagine you are entering the earth at the base of a great old tree. Follow the root structure as if it were a ladder down through the dark earth. At last you will emerge into a beautiful green clearing surrounded by forest. Look around you. At the edge of the clearing you will see the Lord of the Animals sitting on a great tree stump surrounded by his animal friends. Approach him and make your greetings. If he welcomes you, you may continue on your journey. If he does not, then you must return immediately the way you came. When your visit is done, retrace your steps, back into the clearing, saying goodbye to your guide, back up through the dark earth, to the roots of the great tree, and up until once again you are above ground. Open your eyes.

As always, return from your meditative state the way you came, retracing your mental process, the path into the "zone" if you will. Refresh your sense of the literal world with "cakes and ale" and stretch your body gently. Take notes in your journal recording all that you saw and encountered during your meditation. Who or what does your Huascar look like? Describe what you saw. Record your journey now. It is my experience that the details of the meditation journey are sometimes the secret we keep even from ourselves, and like our dreams, if we don't write them down we will forget important details.

You can use the core practice above as a starting point, or make up your own process like I did with the sea otters and kelp bed. Allow your imagination to guide you and embellish the starting scenes so that your attention is captured by your surroundings causing your mind's chatter to subside. Once you have accessed the Lower world, take note of all that you see, it might be important. Who is there? Always access these guides with respect and honor. We are, after all, accessing the mythic: the gods and goddesses who are our models.

Journeying to the worlds takes practice. Make sure that you have plenty of time to refresh and process in between journeys. Practice moving comfortably down to the Lower world several times in this first month of the Huascar archetype. Once you feel secure in the basic journey process, make a totem animal journey so that you can begin to expand your work by following your path with a guide at your side. Like most things that are worthwhile, meditation, particularly journeying between the worlds, takes repeated practice; but soon enough you will be able to slip into that state no matter what the distractions.

Seeing

One of the Celtic images associated with the Lower world is the cauldron. A most famous cauldron discovered in a peat bog in Jutland is known as the Gundestrup Cauldron and among its decorations is an image of a Lower World God. Cauldrons, still ponds, wells, and watery vessels in general have long standing reputations as places available for divination. Later, mirrors (a very modern tool) were used in the same way. Seeing or divination using water or mirrors is powerful and sometimes dangerous work. What we want to recognize here is that water represents a portal to the Lower world.

The Mythology of the Lower World God

We have already mentioned the Celtic Cernunous and the Green Man and the Lady of the Lake. The Celtic mythological record is marred by a distinct lack of written record. All of our mythology for the Celts comes from either Roman observers, historians who were analyzing what they considered a barbarous and dangerous enemy and were anxious to portray that enemy to the political satisfaction of their Roman leaders, or later, a Christian clergy determined to assimilate the pagan Celts into the Christian dogma. The Welsh Mabinogian, the Cycles in Irish texts, and the later heroes such as Arthur and the knights are all second-hand accounts. What we assume and put together of Celtic mythology is therefore some combination of advised speculation. Yet we feel a recognition in these myths, a connection that speaks to us, a sense of knowing that enlarges them beyond the tale-telling of warring nations and their historians. These myths spark a recognition, a re-remembering in us as clearly as throwing an anchor into the sand. We feel to the core of our being a kinship to the mythology that connects us to the universe. What myths speak to you this way?

Often the mythology of the Lower world involves a whole race of people. We have already seen that the Firbolg people were driven underground, and so, the myth goes, appear to us in twilight and darkness as the little people. In Norse lore, Hel, the Norse female god was ruler of the land of the Giants and the realm of the dead.

We can view the three worlds, Lower, Middle and Upper as representations of the cycle of birth, life and death. The Upper world is the realm of potential, of birth waiting to happen. The Middle world is the world of the living, the Lower world that of the dead. There is often associated with the Lower world a god who is perpetually dying. This is the god of the harvest's end, the season of death that must come before renewal. This dying god is held captive in the Lower world until he can be released, completing the circle, back to the world of potential, of birth. The Greek god Adonis was such a god as this, as was Tammuz the Mesopotamian god of vegetation. Innana, the goddess of war, did battle in the underworld in order to restore fertility to the world.

Our Hummingbird journey learns from these myths of the Lower world that life has its cycles. Time is not linear, we find in our bodies and in our spirit that there are ever changing, renewing cycles. The Hummingbird knows, along with all of her fellow creatures except for humans, when to migrate and where to find her nurturing. Her path and time clock are set in her DNA. Birds in their migratory patterns are the most amazing example of the determination with which instinct renews itself from one generation of birds to the next. We humans have to relearn this in each lifetime. This is part of the Hummingbird's path. Within our journey there are moments to rest, to savor our progress, and there are moments for action. We recognize these cycles within our own bodies. We have become rather adept at ignoring or perverting the cycles as they present themselves. We encourage children to dress and act older than their years, and older women are pressured to stay nubile with chemicals and superficial restructuring of their bodies. Women who are able to tune into and learn from the moon phases give themselves the gift of a personal road map. The cycle of the moon is to the woman the same kind of specific set of directions that the snow geese follows in order to return to the tundra. The pressures of growing, learning, being beautiful—these are the challenges that the heroine of the classic myth faces in her quest. Accepting that the path is formed and informed by its cyclic nature is a powerful key to success and survival. We can either follow the path that is our informed destiny, or we can, like Psyche, constantly mirror the broken paths of those around us. In the next chapter we will look at this cycle again in the form of the Triple Goddess.

Exercise:

1. Practice, Practice, Practice. During the month of this archetype, work with your meditation process itself so that you develop a strong pathway to the Lower world. Do a meditation for your personal Totem Animal and then practice taking it with you as you meditate. Add images of your totem animal to your altar.

2. Review the goals you identified in Eagle. How are you bringing your gift into your real world activity? Meditate on the obstacles you have

encountered, and ask your totem animal to help you sort through difficulties so that your objective can be accomplished more easily.

How has your idea of service changed over this month? Are you discouraged? Are you excited by something that has entered your life as a result of your stepping into the world in a way of service? Establish what your next step should be. Where are you in the cycle of this project? As with the new moon, we always begin projects with great enthusiasm and energy, and then we meet a phase of hesitation, even difficulty. What path should you take now? How does the activity you are now involved with mirror your life's journey? As Hummingbird, where have you found the sweetness, the nectar, the joy? Meditate on this question and record your answers in your journal.

6

The Middle World God

Joining the Real World

While it may seem as though this chapter is a chance to relax a little, you will likely find that the work you have done so far has expanded your senses in such a way as to bring you to your every day world in a completely new way. You should be looking at the natural world around you with a sense of integrative depth. You are no longer walking on the earth, you are at one with her. At this point in your meditation work you may be encountering many symbolic images deep within your meditative state, but don't forget to look for meaning in the world around you—the first buds of spring, the flight of birds, an encounter with an animal on the hiking trail. Just at the moment I wrote those words two ravens flew into the oak trees outside my window. I could simply notice, "Oh, two ravens, I don't see them too often." Or I could stop and wonder why? Raven is my daughter's totem animal. Sometimes I see them and she calls or needs me. Why two this time? What does Raven classically mean? If you recall the Norse mythology, Raven is Thought and Memory, the two messenger birds of the god, Odin. Raven works in all levels: in the Middle world he is the thief, attracted to shiny metal objects, and I've noticed he loves to tease. He speaks with more than one voice, a squawking, harassing powerful call and an unearthly clucking he uses for attracting his mate. Because I'm tuned in to my daughter and paying attention to the world around me, it won't surprise me if when I call her later she says, "I was just going to call you." And her news will be important.

I'll tell you another story about how the work we are learning here integrates with the real world. I travel with Jaguar. Shaman's use Jaguar as a tracking animal, and I've used him for many years as I've already shared with you. When I drive off in the car, I ask Jaguar to guide me and protect me. One day I was driving to San Francisco. It's a long, beautiful drive that starts out with about seventy miles of the windiest road in California so the driving is challenging. But then comes the freeway and I can relax. So I was driving down the freeway thinking about other things and only nominally paying attention to the fairly open road ahead of me when suddenly I felt goose bumps all over my body, my hair stood on end, and I sat up straighter in my seat, completely alert. Not two minutes later three cars ahead of me suddenly swerved and parted to leave me heading directly into a box of broken wine bottles strewn across my lane of highway. Without Jaguar's wake-up call I would surely have crashed into the mess on the road, or worse, swerved into the lanes beside me without thinking ahead. Trust me, Jaguar is the best backseat driver anyone can have!

The world of our waking, physical reality is full of information about our Hummingbird journey and the destiny that stands before us. Paying attention to that information is going to mean slowing down, acting deliberately, and honing our ability to read the signs out of the chaos. Obviously, not every little thing is a sign of great import or even a sign at all. Once you begin to pay attention to the cycle of life around you, you will work your way through your world in a completely new and empowered way. Dropping a dozen eggs on the floor just as you were grabbing a bottle of water and running out the door might be an accident, or it might be a deliberate interruption of your too hectic schedule. Or it might save your life.

This chapter is about your world and how well you learn to read its evidence. Our Greek mythological friend, Psyche, couldn't read her world at all. In fact, she was empty headed and vain for the most part although she had the potential to open her heart. *She couldn't act without help.* She was a woman. If we strive, as women or men, to overcome one thing in this world, it should be that women don't need any more or less help than men. It is time to rewrite that archetype. And within that struggle, we as women have to admit that we collude with the old myth because we conspire against one another much as Aphrodite, out of jealousy, conspired against poor Psyche. Recognize now that no matter whether you are man or woman you are on this path alone; that the joy and grace you get from your journey is yours alone to discover. Whether you proceed along the way with a partner or without, it will always be your singular journey. Most of the path will require that you travel on the strength of your own spirit. How well you integrate with the worlds will make the difference between the sad bondage of Psyche and the freedom of Hummingbird. We'll work through this a bit more when we come to our Jungian archetype meditations in the next section.

The ability to read the signs and act rather than be paralyzed by them is learned. Sometimes the hard way. We can overdo. We all know people who won't leave the house without reading their horoscopes, won't fly on Friday the 13th, won't pitch the baseball without scratching their necks. Some of this is good sense, some of it is just how we remind ourselves that we matter. I used to think eclipses were interesting astronomically; but it wasn't until our family suffered a major tragedy during a lunar eclipse that I realized the power of eclipses to effect chaos. Now I chart the dates for each year's annual eclipses, and plan my day accordingly. The moon, after all, is a powerful force.

Bringing the World into Being

As modern Western shaman we accept as one of our goals the idea that we want to create a world of unified and peaceful coexistence among all her creatures. We would recognize the threats posed to the Earth by global warming, overpopulation, and mankind's doctrinaire penchant for wars even without ancient predictions calling us to task. But we feel a sense of urgency and a need to share that urgency with all of our fellow travelers. We must act to change the destiny that the past several hundred years of actions has set as our course. In Eagle we set as our goal to define the acts of service that we personally could effect and we began along our determined path of realization. In the Middle world we ask Spirit to intervene, and then we get ready to respond when Spirit asks us to step up. The Q'ero shaman would say it's time to grow corn. They mean that we work with the earth to grow her bounty, not tear it down. We listen and we nurture, we hope, eventually, that we will reap the harvest of beauty and life, not war and destruction. But growing corn isn't a passive activity that you can watch from afar. We must get out into the fields, grab the hoe and seeds and begin, each of us, in our own way. Part of the reason that the Q'ero shaman, descendants of the Inka, have come down from the high Andes to teach, share, and heal with the lineage of the mountains is that they have divined an urgency to our Fate. For them, 2012 isn't another presidential election year, it's a crisis. But in their elementally positive way, they see that the answer to the crisis we have brought upon ourselves is to grow corn and share the bounty. They will teach us to be shaman because they know that the connections we make with each other will only further our ability to change the destiny of the world from disaster to peace. Heal the world. Grow corn.

The mythology of the Middle world is about separating the sky from the underworld. Some mythology assigns the task of holding up the sky to a god. Egypt's god Nut, for example, is depicted in a mantle of stars holding up the sky so that the world below can exist. For the Q'ero the Middle world god is called Quetzalcoatl. Quetzalcoatl is the White Lord, the Feathered Serpent. He is serpent (earth) and the Quetzal bird (sky) as one. He represents the direction of the West—the place of the setting sun. South Africa has a similar god archetype called Listening Bird. He is the Rainbow Serpent, and his archetype is seen in Australia as well. The cosmic serpent, then. Quetzalcoatl.

There is also an association with fire here. We require fire for our survival on earth, but fire can come from within as well. What do you notice about the activity of service you have planned? Is there an element of Fire in it? Has it become a quest or a cause for you? This fire is connecting you to this world, perhaps for the first time in a meaningful unselfish way. On our personal Hero's journey we all encounter tests, tests of the heart, of communication, of community, of logic. Now is the time to assess your progress. How has your work healed your heart? How has it expanded your ability to communicate what drives your destiny? Where in your community have you unexpectedly found communion, for that is what our community is for. Are you no longer alone on your quest? Are you an army? What has changed in your logical thinking? At what point in your work did you realize that asking the universe for what you want didn't get you anywhere? That the key is working alongside Spirit as guardian to the earth. Balance and synchronicity. When synchronicity happens you get what you need without asking, sometimes without knowing that's what you needed.

How Many Layers Are There?

The cosmology of indeginous peoples varies, of course, but they all agree that there is more to our universe than the world in which we live. Are there three worlds? Are there six? Is there an upper world, a lower world and our own reality plus the four directions? This is what the Inka say. But when we look at the various stories around cosmology we see that generally the number of layers relates directly to two things: the natural world, and the degree of sophisitication within the mythology. Sometimes, this sophistication is the result of thousands of years of accumulated and stored knowledge. The Hindu cosmos, for example, is many layered and peopled by many gods of varying power. People who live by and depend upon the sea, such as the Inuit, base a great portion of their cosmological importance upon the lower world, which they place deep in the sea. Other groups, including the Inka, make a distinction in the worlds by identifying layers within each world. In the Upper world, the second layer is the plant world, this is where shaman go to seek medicine knowledge from the plants themselves, and while this plant world is important for the Inka, it is primary for the Amazonian people who live deep in the jungle. We borrow from the cosmos when we divide the human body into three realms: the lower base nature, the middle instinctive nature, and the mental and spiritual higher planes of the brain. Making these divisions helps us understand and work with our universe.

The Third Eye

Quetzalcoatl, the Middle World god, resides in our sixth chakra at our foreheads. This is where your sixth sense of clairvoyance lies. While your instinct, a more physical response connection between body and mind, your inner warning system, comes from the gut, your third eye is your way of seeing what you draw down from Spirit. It is your information pathway to and from the universe. You are always downloading from Spirit. The question is how do you access this pathway? Like everything else, it takes practice. As shaman we are given ceremonial rites to open our third eye, clear the path. They are like a thunderbolt awakening.

We all have these extra senses. Clairvoyance, clairessence, clair-audience etc. I know one woman who sees colors in words and numbers, a brain wiring science calls synesthesia. There are people who see colors around our bodies. These people have a physical routing in their brains that puts colors to a generally invisible energy. Not all of us have that particular brain wiring, but we do all have third eye capability. If yours has lain dormant for all of your life, now is your chance to wake it up and start using it. Just like meditation, it takes practice and focus. Unless you're an Amazonian shaman, the use of psychedelic drug-related meditation devices are merely fast track pathways to a natural clairvoyance available to each of us; drugs are for people who don't want to do the work. We won't all develop the same extra sensory ability in the same way or to the same degree. It may take some time to recognize your strongest sense.

Recently a book came out aimed at the science-oriented audience that claimed to explain away all the "New Age nonsense" about auras. This book proceeds to explain that we all have energy fields around us that are controlled by our brains, and that there is nothing "whoo-hoo!" about that. Well, of course! Funny how science spends years denying things only to then pretend they just discovered them! It is true that we have an energy field around our bodies that is regulated or interpreted by our brains. In effect, our body is more than just the physical space we occupy. Our sensory ability extends beyond touch into the protective bubble that is our entire energy field. Like clairvoyance, our extra senses work more in the realm of this energy layer than in our physical layer and so are, pardon the expression, more *sensitive*. Whether these additional sensory abilities are well developed brain pathways or gifts from Spirit doesn't matter. What matters is that we use them because we are going to need them. Over stimulation of our ordinary five senses has left us exhausted and permanently functioning in "fight or flight" mode. We need to reduce the stress on our physical bodies because that stress leaves us vulnerable to disease. One important way to reduce this is to develop and then respond to our third eye connection to the universe. This is a real world tool of survival, not a party trick. We have a choice: we can devolve into an early version of humans surviving on fighting over food, sex, and gods, or we can evolve into a species working on the energetic in conjunction with the Universe under a global sensibility. We are currently perilously close to the former mode, warring against one another on a basic survival level—either you die or I die, but one of us has to go. All of us, men and women, have an opportunity to evolve and put these masculine base tendencies to rest in favor of feminine nurturing modalities. This will be the Middle world struggle of this century. Evolve or die out.

The Middle World Altar

What does your perfect world look like? Where do you live and who lives there with you? If there is an artist archetype in you, draw a picture that will form the base for this Quetzalcoatl altar. If not, collect pictures and items that represent your perfect world. Notice as you do this how much of this world already exists for you and how much of it is yet to come. Who are you in your most perfect moment. No "ifs" or conditions required, just who is the perfect you? Think through your roles in life so far. Make a list. Add to the list the roles you would like to have. These roles are Archetypes you have adopted for yourself. Can you narrow the list down to the top eight? My list would include wife, mother, poet, and hermit. These are my archetypes. Choose the one most positive archetype you identify for yourself (reviewing the lists Caroline Myss sets out in her *Sacred Contracts* book is very helpful here) and add something to the center of your altar that represents that archetype. (Working on our shadow archetypes—control freak, bitch, gossip—we'll touch on this later. For now, we are concerned with choosing our best destiny, so we'll avoid worrying about shadow aspects.) When you have your altar arranged around your perfect primary role, spend some time writing in your journal about that role and how, if you are not already manifesting it to your satisfaction, you can work that role into your destiny path.

Since we have said that this Middle world growth period is really about expanding our senses and reading the signs the natural world around us has to give, try to do this meditation outdoors during the day. This might be a challenge for your concentration abilities, but it's important to learn to meditate wherever you are. If you can find a quiet spot in the park, at the beach, or just out in your back yard, plug in your iPod and listen to the meditation poem and then extend your meditation cycle with a conscious opening of your third eye. If you have an inkling of where your strengths lie in your extra sensory ability, give yourself a little cue, "I can see" or "I can hear" or "I can feel" and tap your third eye gently with your fingers before you begin.

This meditation teaches you a physical movement with your hands that opens and expands your energy field. It begins in prayer pose, your hands palm-to-palm in front of your heart, then reach your hands to the sky, turn your palms outward and bring them down to your sides scribing a circle with your arms outstretched, and then returning to meet again in front of your heart. When we open our energy field in this way, we physically invite our extra senses to become active and we signal to our bodies that we are working at the level of the sacred. Prayer pose is a universal gesture linking our own body in a continuous circle as well as signaling an act of the divine. Never be afraid to assume this posture, it is not the right and realm of Western theocracy.

Remember to breathe.

The Quetzalcoatl Meditation

Sit quietly. You are of the earth and sky,
you hear the wind, feel the sun, are washed
with the tears of raindrops.
Let your senses open
and be caressed by this moment, in this world.

Close your eyes.
See and hear with your 6th chakra:
your most important sense of all.

Open the magical chamber of your third eye
to colors so bright and vivid they are almost
unbearable, like the real world we live in.
See me with all your senses.
Sit on your haunches, your head raised
like the serpent about to strike.
Your tail feathers cascade behind you,
a shuddering of resplendent green softness.

Now, as if they are wings,
move your arms into prayer pose,
Arc:
Upward toward the stars and sun and moon,
Outward to the mountains—the apus of your birth
and your becoming,
to the lineage of the Laika,
the wisdom keepers,
Before you in prayer pose to embrace the
immediacy of the present moment.
Now when you open the sacred space around you,
know that your are calling me:
Quetzalcoatl, Lord of the Middle World.

Keep your hands in prayer pose while I tell you
who I am.

I am feathered softness,
feel my wings undulate across your forehead,
let my rainbow of color expand your third eye,
my place of worship.
I am the Quetzal bird, messenger of the gods,
I am sacred, more precious than gold.
My tail is brightest green.
When I fly I am emissary of the Air Dragon clan.
But wait…
I am also Coatl, Serpent,
the Earth Dragon's mistress.
Quetzalcoatl, flight and earth bound
one and the same.
I am the here and now.

I am Quetzalcoatl, Lord of the Middle World,
I am Venus for you,
I bring you the promise of the Morning Star.
I am Lord of the Dawn, the Day Bringer,
seek me out when the first song bird sings.
I am Kokopelli, Kukulkan, Koni Raya, flute player,
fire eater, master of the volcano.
I bring harmony to the Middle world,
I am the Organizer of your real world tasks.
I can empower you to say what needs saying,
master your earthly journey.
I am above and below because I am the air in flight,
and I am slithering at your toes.
I am the right hand of your mestana when you
fold your healing bundle.

I bring you medicine plants and water sources,
I have shown you how to pave your path with sacred stones.
Watch while I dance, my long tail kissing the earth.

I brought you the music of the air—the flute
and of the earth—the drum.
Call on me for knowledge of the myriad ways of
the Earth. This realm.
I am the equilibrium between earth and sky.
Hold your hands before your Third Eye,
I am there.
I am Quetzalcoatl,
Lord of the Middle World.

The Mythology of the Middle World

For Europeans the most widely recognized mythological figure might be Pan, the Greek lord of nature. Pan, perhaps thanks to Shakespeare and *A Midsummer Night's Dream* is a spritely flute-playing fantasy that encourages the child in all of us to remember what the wonders of the natural world really are and how delighted we were as children to use our imaginations without restriction (and without computers). Other representations of Middle world gods are more stern in nature, Geb, the Egyptian ruler of the day and the earth, and even Kokopelli for as lively as his pictorial icon is, he does, after all play with fire and live inside volcanoes.

Most of the important mythology of the Middle world deals with creation stories, cosmology. We've come to take for granted the tripartite nature of the cosmos, that there is a Lower world, a Middle world and an Upper world. One Native American myth tells of the three parts of the turtle representing the three parts of the cosmos. The upper and lower shell of the turtle are the sky and the realm below while the body of the turtle is the world in the middle. The tricksters in mythology, Coyote, Maui, and Pan specialize in moving between the worlds, but they are creatures of the Middle world for whom sexuality, practicality, and cunning are important attributes. Maui made the day longer so that we can cook and prepare our food. Coyote teaches us how to be clever and thoughtful, how to survive. Venus, another goddess of the Middle world, gives us the urge to fall in love and makes being feminine a virtue. There is a practical aspect to these mythological figures, they teach us how to function in real time. They are models, archetypes.

Our journey as Hummingbird within the Middle world is two sided. Hummingbird asks us to look at our real world and respond to the question: Who am I? And then she asks us to open all of our senses, expand, and ask the question again. We must know who we really are before we can step into our becoming, our calling, our destiny. Think about the nature of the word "calling" as it might have been in times before written words. Think about sitting before the fire thousands of years ago, in a deep meditative state, sitting before the fire listening to the call of the natural world deep in the darkness behind us, and the inner voice calling deep in the recesses of our own minds. This is our becoming. We must take our cues from the call of the world around us as well as that inner voice that asks us to achieve our best possibilities.

Exercise:

This is a wonderful exercise we performed as ceremony during our training with The Four Winds Society, and we use it often with our energy medicine clients. It is something all of us should do periodically during our lives.

On small slips of paper list all of your roles (wife, husband, mother, father, sister, lover, teacher, healer, care-giver, friend, student, Queen, damsel in distress, macho guy etc) bad or good, as they come to you, just write them down. Then create a small sacred fire and with ceremony and honoring, burn each slip of paper—ritually casting aside each of those roles. Although you may still need to access the "mommy" role in your life from time to time, by putting it into the fire, you withdraw from being governed by that role. This is a profound ritual, very liberating. Do it with serious intent. Spend some time writing in your journal about how you feel after your ritual fire is completed.

7

The Upper World God

Hummingbird's Highest Purpose

In the course of our journey from our base chakra and Serpent archetype to the connection from our crown chakra to Spirit, we have looked at our personal organization: our past, our current roles, and our aspirations always from the standpoint of self first. The "I" of our relationship with the universe needs to be in balance before we can move on to accessing our highest purpose. We need to have experienced the satisfying touch of synchronicity, to know that the efforts we make outwardly, from "I" to "thou," have connected. We complete this section of work with our crown chakra connection to Spirit and all that that title encompasses. When we open sacred space as shaman we call "to the star nations, Father Sun, Grandmother Moon…" and we acknowledge the unknowable character of Spirit, for in truth, we have no idea how great and vast the connection or character of Spirit is. What we do know is that to achieve our highest purpose in this lifetime we want the pathway between ourselves, *our self*, and Spirit to be open and flowing with power. This, the connection, is the holy grail. This is the purpose of the Hummingbird's journey. We are not, if we are fulfilling our destiny, on an aimless trail without goals. We look for a sense of purpose that threatens to burst from our hearts, a pull so compelling we never lose focus. We are mortal, but we want to live like gods, in dharma, not karma. We want to live thoughtfully and fully.

As Hummingbird, we live at the level of the sacred. We don't have to go through all the hard lessons of life because we've stepped away from the action-reaction behavior of karma and into the sacred, outside of time, where we stay in right relationship, in balance, with self, with our fellow creatures, with the universe. We ask for our highest destiny not for ourselves, not for mankind, but for all the universe, and when we meet with Spirit as Hummingbird we surrender to the sacred journey.

Traditionally, the crown, or seventh chakra, is seen as our connection to the universe, from the top of our skull reaching up to the sky. This is where we receive divine inspiration, where we access divine purpose. It is our umbilical cord to the great unknown universal being from which we spring and to which we will all return. This is where the gods contact us, where we are asked to be greater than our simple selves. The great 15th century Inka leader, Pachacutec, lends his name to this archetype, Pachacuti, meaning "world-turner" or "world-transformer," or in Quechua, "he who changes the world." He is Lord of the Dawn, Lord of our Becoming. This is where we step into the destiny we are meant to follow. This is where we will transform the service goal we began in Eagle into a divine journey, where Hummingbird challenges us to drop "I" and adopt "we" because when we say "yes" to the universe and to our destiny on her behalf, everything we need comes to us while we are busy serving the needs of the greater world. The divine journey can alter the course of our planet. This is our ultimate potential.

We have asked ourselves in this work from first to seventh chakra, from Serpent archetype to Pachacuti archetype, to redefine the classic Hero's grail quest. We are no longer interested in whether Psyche can unlearn vanity and stand on her own two feet. We are not interested in cunning, lying, deceiving or prostituting our way into a future we cannot begin to understand. That's the old dynamic. We are firmly on the path of Hummingbird, and we know the sweetness of that journey. We are building knowledge with every stop and every flight, and we know that the path is our finest choice because we have taken the road at the level of the sacred. We have put our hearts and spirits on the line.

Imagine a pin ball machine. In the old pattern, the creator pulled the plunger back and out we sailed, first a long and airy trajectory of childhood and then, Wham! Suddenly everything began to change as we bounced and smacked our way up, down and sideways through our lives, sometimes lingering in one pocket of safety or another only to be given a good whack and off we go again, no known destination and absolutely no control. In the new pattern, we consider our past and set it aside, lessons learned. Then we consider our future, what do we want most for our world and what part can we take in making that desire come about? We want to throw out a line, a definition, our highest aspirations, like a mountain climber chucking a line up to the top peak. Now that we have the line, all we have to do is move upward along it. All it takes is one line well thrown and a toe hold. And remember, don't look down!

The Realms of the Upper World

Remember when we said "as above, so below" about the Middle world? Well, the Upper world might be seen as "as below, so above." All that is in the literal world of our everyday existence is mirrored in the realms of the Upper world. Imagine it as levels: first the Stone world where all matter began. Stones are the ancient ones, the oldest things in the universe. Then comes the Plant world. When the Amazonian shaman take the hallucinogenic plant mixture auyahuasca they do it to seek out the plant world and ask for medicine inspiration. The shaman works in the Plant world to gain knowledge of the DNA of plants, the spirit of plants, and they bring back that knowledge to work with their patients. If you ask a healer how he knew what plant would cure an illness, he would say that the plant told him. We can make a meditative journey here to find our own personal plant medicine.

Above the Plant world is the Animal world, where the essence of all animals resides. Animals as Archetypes. Just as we can journey to the Lower world for totem animals, we can also come here to find them.

Above the Animal world is the world of our Ancestors: archangels, guides, and the spirits of our ancestors are here. And above that place where we all return, is the world of our Becoming, the world of our possibility. When we meditate for a new destiny line, we come and seek it here.

The Upper World Altar

How does it look to make the journey into the Upper world? By now you have been honing your meditation skills for several months. You should be able to journey to the Lower world with ease, and you should be able to work in the Middle world caring for and interacting with the plants and animals in new and deeper ways. In order to create your Upper world altar you will make a meditative journey to the Upper world and identify symbols from each realm you visit. Rather than do this after the chapter meditation and have your journey crowded with images taken from that meditation, you're going to do the Altar meditation first. I want what you see to be wholly your own. Wherever you are led on this journey, whether it be a lush garden, a silver castle in the stars, or a galactic, planet-hopping, surprise party, this meditation belongs to you. This will be your Upper world landscape; let it flow from your imagination knowing that imagination stems from your memory, your remembering, of all the lifetimes of knowledge you have collected and stored in your subconscious.

Upper World Journey

Settle yourself in your quiet space, either darkened or with a single focus candle if you still need a visual aid to keep your mind from wandering.

Begin your session with breathing. Take as long as you need to calm your physical self and empty your mind of the day's trivia. If you have trouble doing this, just take your time, breathe deeply, and relax. Eventually you will be ready. Take a deep breath and ask Hummingbird to be a totem animal for this journey. Feel her come to your side.

When you are ready to begin your journey you need only remember these things:

1. You are going up. Don't get lost!
2. There are Five Realms to visit: Stone, Plant, Animal, Ancestor, Becoming
3. You are only a visitor checking out the landscape. Do not engage actively with any of the creatures or spirits you might see.

Begin the Journey

As you begin your ascent to the Upper world notice your surroundings. Follow Hummingbird's lead. What is the path and where is it taking you? Don't busy your mind questioning what you see, accept it, commit it to memory, re-remember it, you have been here before. As you stop at each realm of the Upper world, just observe what you see, as if you are standing at the doorway, not engaging. Then move on. You are mapping the landscape on this journey, you are not interacting with anyone or anything you see along the way.

When you have visited all five realms, return down to the earth the way you came, bringing Hummingbird with you. Write in your journal a thorough description of all of the realms and how you got there. Think about each realm in turn and find something you saw in that realm that you can now symbolically represent on your altar. Build your altar to the Upper world and prepare for the Pachacuti Meditation.

Becoming Hummingbird

The Upper World holds our past as well as our future. It holds potential, it holds our Becoming. The Q'ero shaman say we will soon have an opportunity to evolve, to become. Our becoming as Hummingbird comes down to us from the fifth realm of the Upper world. When we're ready, that is where we will go to map our destiny at the level of the sacred. Then, like Pachacuti himself, we will turn the world over. The Q'ero say the world has been upside-down for five hundred years. For them 2012 is the turning point, the time for things to right themselves.

There are many ways to discover our sacred journey—Mother Teresa found hers in Calcutta, the Dalai Lama's found him as a young boy. Most of us don't ever do anything so grand or spiritual, but each of us can have a journey that takes us to the level of the sacred even while we produce the mundane in order to survive. I know someone who divorced her entire family and went off on a walkabout, filled with a self importance that must have made her family shake their heads in wonder. Perhaps she will complete her personal work someday and get to the real point of this project called life, but what I'm asking you to do is not reject your "life so far" unless it has been truly ghastly and needs rejecting for survival reasons. This is not an invitation to delve more deeply into the dysfunction of your life. On the contrary, I'm asking you to step above the mundane so that you can nurture the life you have from a level of the sacred, from the level of the profound and universal "we"—so that you drink from the nectar of stillness and wonder, and every day you find grace in the journey and solidarity in the companionship of your fellow travelers.

When you are ready, sit before your altar and listen to or recite the Pachacuti Meditation. Let all of the sacred archetypes be present with you as you accept this lord of the Upper world into your crown chakra. We, together, are becoming Hummingbird.

The Pachacuti Meditation

Dreams are made in my world.
When we dream we send the seeds of our destiny
into the Upper World,
the world of becoming: the world of Pachacuti.
The Spinner.
We cast our chances many times
as children of the world
before we see that the line of our true destiny
is ours to call,
and call it we must or face the chaos of a world
determined by the past.

I am
Pacha kutiq, world-turner, world-transformer.
In history, my name belonged to the ninth Inka of
the Kingdom of Cuzco.
I am the power of the destroyer,
the creator, re-turning history.
I am here to demand change.
To exalt in a new world.
I bring you access to the ancestors,
guardian angels, archangels, and spirit guides.
Who calls you? Whom do you seek?

Come across my worlds,
a silver glittering staircase ascending,
seek me within the oldest regions of the stones
all grey matter, stark and rigid.
All life begins here.
Seek me within the plants,
come here for ancient wisdom,
for your personal medicine,
all healing begins here.

Come up to the animal plane,
here are the betweens
—stay unattached as you visit here—
seek only the animals that will guide your path.
Come here to assist the dead
recapitulation begins here.

Come by my side,
I am Pachacuti, lord of the Upper world,
at my right and my left are the archangels
of all beliefs.
Around me and below me
as far as the eye and heart can see
are the ancestors.
Tripping out into the star nations,
the galaxies beyond and within,
let go of your linear mind and follow us
we will lead you in the great spiral dance.

Join hands,
Prepare for the turning time.
Prepare for Pachacuti.

Archangels

Spirit guides, guardian angels, archangels, fairies—all of these helpers come down to us from the Upper world. Archangels are powerful defenders and their ancient and timeless wisdom has elevated them to this exalted position. Perhaps they were creator gods, or perhaps they were humans of extraordinary grace and wisdom who have stepped beyond earthly lifetimes in order to assist us. They can be valued allies. You can use your meditation skills to journey to the Upper world expressly to meet an archangel to work with you.

The Mythology of the Upper World

I love the mythology of Thunder, perhaps the strongest Upper world archetype around. Thunder, unseen and all powerful. Lightning, the weapon of awakening, of inspiration. They say shaman are often chosen for their profession by being struck by lightning. A bolt from above. The Q'ero shaman joke that that's just for those people who weren't paying attention to the first seven or eight signs of their destiny. Let's hope we don't have to be struck by lightning in order to get the message. Thor. Thunderbird. Zeus. Taranis. Ilyap'a, Perun, Susano, Hadad are some of the names of the gods of Thunder. Raven, eagle, and reindeer are animals of the Upper world. Our Santa Claus sleigh pulled by reindeer probably comes to us from the Arctic mythology that gives these animals the archetypal qualities of the messenger. Flight is an attribute of the Upper world. In communist Russia, there was an official police effort to eliminate all shaman from the indigenous cultures in Siberia. Sometimes shaman would be taken up in airplanes and thrown out to their deaths in order to prove that shaman can't fly.

There are some who think the Thunder is a woodpecker. Woodpeckers are powerful totem animals with strong affinities for shaman's drums and they are associated with the head and crown, the crown chakra as well as the third eye. The tapping of the woodpecker is tapping open the extra senses. Drumming is often seen as a gateway to using our extra sensory abilities by its trance inducing tones. In Greek mythology the woodpecker is associated with Zeus, the god of thunder and with Mars, the god of war, drumming soldiers into battle.

Creator gods come from the Upper world—Great Spirit, Father Sun, Grandmother Moon. In one African culture the creator moon is male, not female. For the Iroquois the creator gods of the Sky sent down the first ancestor, Ataensic, a woman who came down from the Upper world and is the mother of us all.

The Work of Becoming

Transforming the work of your life into sacred action is as simple as this: When you can answer the question, "Why are you doing that?" with "Because the world needs it done" you have done your work. When you can take the "I" out of the journey, connect your spirit to the divine feminine of the Earth, of Pachamama in such a way that you live the fine details of your everyday life wholly conscious of the actions and reactions, the implications each act has upon the universe, then you live at the sacred.

You began with divesting yourself of your "issues" by forgiving, forgiving yourself and forgiving those who you feel have wronged you. Then you armed yourself with the power of guides and newly awakened senses so that you were completely aware of your connection to the universe. You chose your starting point and began the magical transformation. You took wing.

Different hummingbirds fly in different patterns and they can be identified by the arc and swing of their flight. The birds in my garden nest at the very top of 150 foot tall pine trees. All summer long they swoop in and out of the garden, darting past us as they feed on roses, fuchsia and hydrangea. Their return flight up to their nests never varies, two arcs, three long quick darts. Sometimes they sit in the fuchsia tree amid hundreds of blossoms as if they have emitted a big sigh of pleasure at all of the nectar at their disposal.

Our winged journey may not outwardly change very much from what we have always done, but the way we bring ourselves to the project of life and to our planet and solar system must. If we are to thrive as a planet, we must all change at the core of our beings. We have been working from the subjective: what do *I* want, "not in my back yard"—we need to come up with a term for what is to come—for the time when we work for the earth and all of her creatures. It's not a subjective view, or an objective view (for if we were objective, we might lose heart). What shall we call it?

Exercise:

You are on your developing path of service. Spirit has called and you have answered. Make a new sand painting representing a new mythology for the Earth. Who are your guides, angels, gods? Where is your place among them? Draw, paint, or work in the earth or sand and take some considered time to develop your vision. What paths become available in your world mythology? What people survive and stand with you on your journey? Take a look at the beautiful sand paintings the Hopi create and see how the images within integrate. Sometimes the original healing messages of these paintings have been lost. Use your senses to imagine new meanings and reinvent symbols for your own work. Re-remember the tasks of guardianship. You might want to create your work on paper and hang it on your wall so that over time you can add to it. You might want to do the work all in one day, in sand, and then with deepest ceremony, let the ocean waves take your work out with the tide, out into the sacred.

Write in your journal about the feelings you had while making your sand painting. Can you think of a name for this new mythology? This new way of becoming? Let me know.

Part Two

Defining the Self

Jung, Tarot, and Astrology

The Hero's Journey

Joseph Campbell brought the concept of the Hero's journey back into our awareness with his widely popular analysis of mythology, and his conclusion, his advice for us all "to follow your bliss," was the culmination of assessing the archetypal "grail quest" that we are also using to describe the Hummingbird's journey here. The idea is that the Hero, or Heroine, begins as an innocent and proceeds toward enlightenment, following various paths along the way, and is led or influenced by his or her own growth as well as external archetypal forces. The degree to which we, as Heroes, negotiate the journey with grace depends on our reasoning and our connection to both ourselves, our *self* and Spirit.

Campbell was interested in mythology as an anthropologist first and a psychologist second. Carl Jung came at the same subject in the reverse priority. For Jung, it was imperative in understanding the *self* to understand the archetypes, the "indelible meanings" as he put it, governing that self; and those archetypes were integral to the development of the self—that is, the journey of the Hero. Underneath every action was a governing model.

Angeles Arrien, a renowned tarot scholar, calls the tarot a "psycho-mythological manual." A far more sophisticated application of the tarot than mere divination, the cards serve as a map of all aspects of consciousness (conscious, subconscious, and super-conscious) at the level of the sacred, the level of the Archetypal, the models by which and through which we progress from uninformed child to critically thinking, productive adult. In the same way that we use sand paintings or mandalas to express situations as visual images in order to take them out of ourselves and work them on a mythic level, we use tarot to transform our understanding of our path with images. The aim is the same, to work out our destiny at the level of myth, of the sacred connection.

The Shadow Archetypes

As we have mentioned earlier in the Introduction, Jung identified four archetypes of behavior that we all share. These archetypes are Child, Saboteur, Prostitute, and Victim. We fall into these archetypal patterns as easily as we drive a car. When we make bargains that undermine our own authority we call on Prostitute; when we play the "I'm just a girl" card we call on Victim. It might not be pretty, but we all do it and with regular frequency. But the question is, do we have to? If we are truly on the Hummingbird path, do we ever have to bargain from our shadow side again?

Now that we have embedded the seven archetypes into our chakras we are ready to disengage ourselves from the old way of being and step into our power. To understand the disengagement process we are going to experience four additional meditations, meditations that reach to the core of old patterns of behavior, patterns we might now like to think of as belonging to a species we are about to leave behind as we continue to evolve. These old patterns trap us in a messy, backward looking entanglement from which we can fly if we agree to transform them, shed them, and step out into the void. The poet David Whyte speaks of stepping away from "conversations that are too small for you." We recognize these instantly, don't we? And yet, sometimes we need a nudge to force ourselves to make the brave act that truly feeds our spirit, truly makes us powerful.

The archetype meditations that follow aim to transform the four core Jungian archetypes of Child, Saboteur, Prostitute and Victim into positive models using four of the twenty-two Major Arcana Tarot cards.

Before we do that, we should look at how the tarot's Major Arcana cards work and learn a little about the history of the development of the four cards we have chosen.

The Tarot Cycle

Tarot cards are composed of two parts: the Major Arcana (Arcana is merely a title derived from the word *arcane* meaning secret or hidden) and the Minor Arcana. The Minor Arcana comprise four suits of twelve cards that very much resemble a normal deck of gaming cards except that the four suits are called coins, wands, swords, and cups instead of spades, hearts, clubs, and diamonds. Each suit is given an emphasis or area of consideration. For example, cups deal with love and personal relationships, coins with financial issues. These suits can also be identified by way of Jung's four personality functions, thus swords = thinking, cups = feeling, wands = intuition, and coins = sensation. The court cards (King, Queen, Knight, Page) of all four suits have equivalent representatives in the resulting sixteen Jungian personality type combinations in the Myers-Briggs Type Indicator test.

Jung said, "...the set of pictures in the tarot cards were distantly descended from the archetypes of transformation." He further noted the connection between the notion of the "collective unconscious" (Jung's primary ontological concept) and the Major Arcana cards. How far Jung went in drafting comparisons and uses in tarot is the subject of considerable scholarship. For us, we are concerned only with four of the Major Arcana cards.

The Major Arcana cards are very different from the four suits of the Minor Arcana. Here we find twenty-two cards beginning with 0 and ending with card number 21. Card 0, occurring unnumbered in some decks, is known as the "significator" card and represents the self. Cards 1 through 21 are generally seen as being arranged in three cycles, or what we might call evolutions, each containing seven cards. The cycles seem to be tuned to a process of personal illumination, of growth, and are often interpreted from the idea of the Hero's journey. The Hero begins his journey portrayed as card 0, The Fool, and ends his progress toward "bliss" with card 21, The World. Working with the tarot cards in this way takes common divination to a far higher and more illuminating level.

The three cycles, or parts of the path, formed by the twenty-one cards, plus the 0 card, The Fool, are the base keystones of the Hero's journey. The first seven card cycle can represent the baser instincts for survival, power, appetite. The second seven card cycle deals with mortality, learning life's lessons, and the third cycle follows the path in the spiritual quest, the mystical path. The Fool walks through all twenty-one cards at one time or another. The three paths can also be viewed as the three layers of consciousness. We draw the cards to illuminate those parts of our consciousness that are not revealed in the temporal world. It's another way to peel the onion that is our self.

We are going to take only four of the steps that these cards represent and use them as meditations for our journey. I've chosen these four cards because of the way they relate to Jungian shadow archetypes. When you have completed the twelve meditations here you might want to expand your journey to include a full process of all twenty-two cards. For the time being, we begin at the beginning again with The Fool.

The Fool is the Hero/Heroine of the journey and it is the first meditation in this section. We will regress in The Fool to touch the aspect of the Child archetype that we need to keep as Hummingbird, that is, the notion of *joy*, and to heal and release the shadow Child. In other words, we want to nurture the Divine Child, and leave the wild brat behind.

The numbered card following The Fool is The Magician in the position of 1. For us The Magician will transform The Saboteur, so that what we put our energy to is creation not destruction, truth not deception. So that we survive with *grace*; and Spirit always gives us what we need.

The Lovers, card 6, covers the shadow Prostitute. If we *love* ourselves as strongly as we desire to be loved, we will never betray our spirit or our destiny.

And finally, Justice, card 11, replaces the Victim. If we are in right relationship with ourselves and with the world, we are never the victim, we are always in the right place at the right time, in balance and *harmony*, and the give and take with Spirit is synchronous.

Jung used the four core Archetypes of Child, Saboteur, Victim and Prostitute to peel away the behavior mechanism that caused his clients discord; they are the dark archetypes of the most basic behaviors. We understand that these archetypes are not the positive reflective model. We want to keep a sense of the child-like in our attitude, but we don't want to be childish. In the alchemical tradition, Jung looked at the light side and the shadow side. We want to work out the shadow aspect and realize that the journey is long enough without trying to negotiate the voyage from a position of Prostitute! Part of our evolution as luminous beings is to leave these shadow models behind and step into the light Archetypes that align us with balance instead of struggle at all times.

In the four meditations that follow we will peel away another layer of our old way of being and expose the new face of the four core Archetypes. Complementing these four Jungian concepts of shadow behavior, Caroline Myss in her work *Sacred Contracts* suggests that we add eight more. Let's look at sweet Psyche again and her pathetic trial at the hands of Aphrodite. Psyche is not a brain surgeon; I think we can all see that. Psyche is beautiful and a bit of an airhead. Psyche should probably pick Damsel in Distress as one of her optional Archetypes, right? She's such a "girl." What about Aphrodite? She's Goddess, Queen, Witch, Control Freak, what else? What about yourself? Can you easily choose a few Archetypes that describe you? These don't have to be negative, and that's the point of them for us.

Exercise:

In your journal, make a list of archetypes that you think describe you, but put all of the positive ones (Caregiver, Mom, Leader, Coach, Inventor, Prince) in one list and on another part of your page list all the negative ones (Bitch, Wicked Witch, Crybaby, Bully, Control Freak, etc). In a column next to this list of negative archetypes, list the four core Jungian titles: Child, Victim, Prostitute and Saboteur. Now look at the first title on your personal negative list. Which of the four core archetypes does it represent? Draw a line from the one to the other. Did you end up with more of your lines going to a single particular core archetype?

Now look at your list of positive archetypes. Think about how these archetypes help move you forward on your Hummingbird path. How does each now contribute to reeling in the destiny that is your "bliss"? Which archetype strikes a strong chord of recognition, and which one seems to be fading away? Spend some time writing about the archetypes that were most prominent in your list. Can you cite instances where you had clear choices between the light and the shadow aspects? Which way did you go and what were the consequences? Can you see a pattern in circumstances of stress where your fall back position is one of light or of shadow? We'll come back to this list when we get to Meditation Twelve, your final personal journey.

The Fool

The Card

We begin with The Fool, the tarot card that generally is either not numbered at all, or is numbered 0. Although the card sometimes falls at the end of the twenty-two card Major Arcana, usually it is the beginning card and so it suits us perfectly as the mirror to the Child archetype. In my favorite depiction of The Fool card in Kat Black's Golden Tarot deck, The Fool is dressed in Medieval full-skirted dress and she is playing a drum while she skips along the edge of a cliff, her dog nipping at her heals. There is joyful, innocent, guileless, cautionless, and almost aimless energy all over this card. She stands at the precipice without looking down. Who but a child could do that? Even her dog knows better and nips at her heals to get her to look, but she does not. Like the child, The Fool is not intentionally destructive. The child is not yet a thinking, logical being. The child is completely "I" centered as any of us who have been parents know. The Fool is also not conscious of danger in any way, not from ignorance, but from a childlike perspective. The Child in us is always shocked that we could be threatened. The Fool is generally depicted at the edge of a cliff or top of a mountain symbolizing the aspect of the novice, the beginner. The journey is about to begin, The Fool about to step off into the unknown, and at this moment, he is without fear. This is the aspect we want from The Fool for our Hummingbird journey—stepping onto the path without fear, but with joyful innocence.

The card for The Fool is generally associated with the element Air and so our Hummingbird is enticed to leap, to fly from the edge, to take a chance without fear. It is a moment to embody childlike innocence because that faith, that innocent belief in oneself as invincible, is exactly the kind of courage we need to strike out without hesitation on this new path for our own powerful destiny. Rather than look at The Child as vulnerable, and The Fool as foolish, we will embrace this combined archetype as the Divine Child who represents the birth of new beginnings and bright, daring ideas.

The Divine Child will succeed not by struggle but rather by guile and playfulness. She moves along her path enveloped in a feeling of bliss not because she is ignorant but because she has tasted the bitterness of false paths and now knows the joy of the sweet journey of the heart.

In some tarot decks there is a raven depicted in the scene of The Fool, raven representing the beginning of an inner quest, of accessing one's interior, personal power, personal knowledge. We want to reach deeply into our own magic and learn to fly. We want to understand the moment of separation between spirit and matter, and we can begin to do that by embodying Hummingbird. Hummingbirds defy gravity and the laws of science with their flight. They are focused movement. Like The Fool, Hummingbird is only motivated by the needs of the moment, but the key is that the moment is always about the sweetness of the journey. Always. If you are lost in the details and those details are dragging you under, you have stepped off the path. The Fool and The Child are at the moment of beginning, they are not yet on the Hero's quest. In some tarot interpretations the entire remaining twenty-one card sequence is called The Fool's Journey. Like a child, The Fool is harmless and fearless. She can talk to kings and beggars alike without blame or fear, and she brings to them a child's wisdom. She can speak out because her words come from a place of divine innocence. My two year old granddaughter swung open the back door bare-assed naked and declared, "I'm going out into the World!" perfectly describing the optimistic enthusiasm for the journey ahead that we are all after and that is embodied by The Fool.

The Jungian Child

The simple description of the Child archetype is, of course, the exasperating person who "won't grow up." This person doesn't follow the rules, either at all, or well enough for us to trust in his ability to make logical decisions and follow through. But the real shadow Child archetype is more subtle than that. We use our shadow Child when we pretend to be vulnerable in order to avoid something we don't want to face. Many of our childhood fears brought along with us into adulthood are from the Child, and if we think about them we see that they are unrealistic, that is, they are fears we have not tested in real life. I'm terrified of snakes having had a childhood encounter with a dead garter snake. It was unrealistic then and it's unrealistic now, but I cling to my fear. It justifies my fussiness at camping just anywhere and my over protectiveness as a mother. The funny thing is that now, the moment I think about snakes, I see one, because serpent always arrives when I call her.

Generally, our shadow Child archetype, the darker manifestation of The Child, is a pretty non-threatening state because children may not always be sweet, tidy, and innocent, but we can't say they are powerful; on the contrary, they are always vulnerable. So, what about Jung's positive Child, light Child? Caroline Myss helpfully separates the archetype into multiple categories, refining our insights.

For our purposes let's look at four of the light qualities described by Myss, and see which of the four you will recognize as yourself. The Nature Child, The Eternal Child, Magical Child and Divine Child. These don't really need a lot of picking apart to understand, do they? The Nature Child is the adult who loves more than anything to be out on the hiking trail exploring, bird watching, identifying flowers—this isn't the hiker clocking miles (that's the Eternal Child trying to remain young), this is the person who cannot survive in a city. The Eternal Child still goes to rock concerts, takes up new life affirming hobbies with more frequency and fervor than the rest of us and brings optimism to life. The Magical Child never stops talking to her invisible friends, seeks out the occult and mysterious and sees stars rather than stairs when she looks up. The Divine Child might grow up to be a nun, or she might simply radiate grace; these are the people who have a serenity we can see in their eyes.

Have you got yours picked out? We want to take our Child archetype with us on the journey transformed as The Fool. How you step onto the path of your most perfect destiny, the character or tone of that first step, is defined by your Child archetype. If you have had trouble identifying the act of service you would engage when you were working your Eagle archetype, The Child will give you clues. Are you the Nature Child? Your act of service probably involves environmental stewardship. If you are the Magical Child you might want to train as a shaman and learn the work of energy medicine. If you are the Divine Child you might spend your time in serious devotion, praying for peace.

The Fool steps along the edge, takes chances without hesitation, confident that she has all that she needs, her bundle of things that will keep her alive is tied on a stick or wrapped in a shawl at her side, her dog acts as companion so that she won't be lonely on the path and also as her conscious minder—the dog won't let her go over the edge. What is the scene you see for yourself?

Exercise:

Spend some time deciding which Child archetype you most resemble. If you need to, take the time here to work through the archetype process in *Sacred Contracts: The Journey* (Hay House Publishing), it will help you with the next four meditations.

Draw a picture, your own new tarot card of The Fool. (You will do this for all of the rest of the meditations, so either do this in your journal, or on cardboard cards that you can post on your altar.) Draw yourself as The Fool/Child and include the characteristics and representations accorded to your particular Child. What do you need to have with you in order to be free to step onto the path that is your destiny? What is in the bundle of things you have to have at your side? If you hate your drawing ability, do your best, you'll be surprised, and give yourself permission to write lists around the edge of the card to augment your drawing so that you will remember all that you need.

The Fool Altar

Prepare your altar around the card image you have drawn, collecting together some of the things you will need to keep you safe on your journey, but also to help you retain the innocence and excitement of a child, the joy that will sustain you. Pay particular attention to the things you "cannot live without." Some of these things may not be all that necessary but others, like your family, or your best friend, or your dog might be extremely important to the success of your destiny.

When your altar is ready, prepare yourself in the usual way that you have developed in your ongoing meditation practice. Dress the part: Put on your Divine Child or your Nature Child, go all the way with this, like you would have when you were small, not caring how many layers of leggings or how much glitter you have put on—really allow your Child the freedom to choose. Remember that The Fool at court entertaining before the King dressed ridiculously so that the truths that he spoke audaciously would not meet with rejection or violence. Cloak yourself in The Child, put your truths in the language of innocence and see how easily they will be met with enthusiasm. When my granddaughter declared her intention to step out into the world undressed, her mother didn't say, "No you're not!" She said, "Wait, I'm coming with you!" She knew this was a moment of joy that they could share together and that there would be other steps, many other steps, later on in life that her child would take on her own.

When you have dressed for the first step of your journey, begin the meditation with your breathing. You will notice that the meditations in Part Two are in a different voice. This is you, your interior unconscious call, as if the archetype has stepped outside of you for a moment and is instructing your inner self.

The Fool Meditation

Like Ulysses this journey is your questing as
innocence.
You are pure Joy, the glad heart of a new flower,
the expectation of birthday parties, of laughter
unbound.
You are ready to take your sacred bundle and step
step onto the path of destiny.
Even you can save the world. It's in your attitude,
the manner of your coming.
As you walk onto your path feel the wind caress
your face with the blush of new ideas,
the tricks of your new trade.

You are The Fool, The Beginner, The Innocent.
With you everything is possible,
edges and boundaries are gone.
You are innocence,
the place of nothing that is not empty;
but is only waiting to be filled.
You are no threat, all possibility and play.
Those who would think you mad do envy you.
Now you will be the perfect circle,
time that is not linear
but has looped back on itself
to bring you to this moment,
this mystical quest.

You are The Beginner again,
birthing new ideas.
You are quick, guileless, blissful.
Spread the wings of your personal grand plan.
Dip into your bag of tricks, your pure potential,
what do you find?

With the cleverness of a child unbound,
what do you see?
What is your first step?
Where is the sweetness that will nurture you on
the way?

You are the element of Air:
Breathe,
inhale,
fill your lungs with simple Joy,
Exhale,
send Joy to the World.

The Mythology of The Fool

While Ulysses, the Hero of *The Odyssey* might be the most well recognized Fool archetype, there are several from the Celtic mythology that provide us with more depth regarding the quest for the Holy Grail. In an Arthurian depiction of The Fool tarot card, we would interpret the stick with The Fool's bag of tricks tied to it as the magic wand and the chalice. The Holy Grail, the Chalice, might be seen as our interior chalice, the divine within us all. When we seek it externally, we are looking in the wrong place. From the magic wand will come Inspiration with a capital I, the divine knowing, the spark that will lead us to our grand purpose. Make no mistake, when we reach for the purpose that takes us into service for the universe, it is indeed grand. In the Celtic mythology, the image of The Fool is accompanied by a black dog and a hen, meaning that as The Fool steps off onto his journey he is accompanied by both god and goddess. In the mythology of the Welsh texts, knowledge is what is sought. Knowledge rests ultimately deep within us, in the ancient coded information of our birth. The Grail source of wisdom held by the Celtic Salmon of Knowledge is within ourselves, but our journey toward self knowledge always involves external conflict and accidental foresight. Even the creation of the wisdom seems accidental: in the tale we find the youth given the task of stirring the great cauldron and when he stirs haphazardly, three drops of knowledge splash into his mouth. Suddenly he is no longer the simple child set to stir the soup, now he is the keeper of wisdom and pursued by all others. In his escape, the child takes on the protective guise of many different totem animals, each one bearing a lesson about life and negotiating the journey. The child/Hero learns as he is pursued, but he always possesses the sacred knowledge, he has possessed it all along. The question is, can he keep it?

The Problem with Poor Psyche

Once we have uncovered what we know as our personal truth, our bliss, we can begin our Hero's journey. The journey isn't the search for the answer to the question, "What is my bliss?" You already have that within you. If we peel away the layers, it will reveal itself to us. The journey is the struggle to affect our destiny to its fullest degree, to gather around us the guides who can help us on our path, to refine our purpose so that we can accomplish the tasks before us. If we read about Psyche's struggles to please the Goddess Aphrodite (Venus) we recognize that most of the tasks set for her are impossible ones, and she doesn't set them for herself; they are set for her by the gods. We want to avoid that victim/perpetrator way of being. Although there are many messages encoded in the story of Psyche, the one we want to unpack is the progress of her quest. In the tradition of the story, Psyche, as Heroine, is endlessly and irritatingly mortal. She can't come up with a viable solution to the impediments to her journey on her own. At one point, she needs to visit the Underworld in order to ask Persephone for the gift of Beauty to bring to Aphrodite. The only way she can think to get there is to die, and so she climbs to a great height in order to throw herself off. At every turn, Psyche makes the wrong decision and is stopped from following through by all manner of creatures, helpers, and gods. We see Psyche as Victim, dependent, and we'll encounter this aspect of her again when we work the Meditation Justice and seek to empower Psyche with self-fulfillment. The problem with Psyche's whole story rests in the stance that she represents from the very beginning, that of reactive mortal, not Heroine. If we peel off the morality tale of Ancient Greece that might be proscribing independence, vanity, or thinking outside the box on the part of women, what are we left with? Not much. In fact, we are left with a chilling image of the skeleton of womankind as helpless and inter-destructive. Not only are we not able to help ourselves, but we undermine the progress we see in others. Is this how we want the myth to work in the 21st century? What about the Hero's journey from the mortal male aspect? Is the Hero compelled to do battle throughout the cycle? Must he be doomed to never understand love? Is there an alternative to might or cunning as his primary aspect?

We are standing on the path, confident that the knowledge we seek is contained within us, that the destiny we desire is stretched out before us. Now, we need to know how to transform reality into the high purpose of the Sacred. Into *Grace*.

Exercise:

Redefine the terms "Hero" and "Heroine." Do you notice a difference between the word Hero and the feminine version of the same word? Make a list of Hero attributes on one side of the page in your journal. List the feminine Heroine attributes on the other. Cross out all the negative attributes on either side. What is left? How have you redefined the word? If you are the Hero, are there aspects you would like to change in the meaning of the title for you? If you are the Heroine of your story which single word is the most important one in the definition? Can you see why? Does that one word give you any clues as to how completely you have stepped onto the path of Hummingbird with childlike joy? Does it imply vulnerability or a sense of being stuck? Can you unravel the thread and clear it back to the source so that you can take the next step on your journey?

9

The Magician

The Card

Knowledge is power. This is the force of the first step on the Hero's path. The Magician brings with it all of the unseen magical forces that we are born with, forces to which as children we sometimes have greater access than we are allowed as adults. The power is internal, it is encoded in our DNA, it is in the expansion of our senses. The tarot card in the position of number 1 reminds us of the ordered universe, of the elemental state in which we function and the transformative power of our own place within that system. The Magician makes order out of chaos by connecting the elements, by *alchemy*. The first lesson of The Fool/Hero/Heroine is to recognize that every thing is in some sense alive and interconnected. No action occurs in a void. The life force is all around us, in the trees, animals, stones, earth, and in ourselves. The Magician uses every element available to move forward on his path.

In the famous Sola Busca Tarot deck, The Magician card's meaning is "honesty of intention, and desire for the spiritual." Integrity is the primary ingredient of the alchemy of the soul (Alchemy here meaning "the dazzling transfiguration of the grace that stimulates the intellect."). The creative fire, the muse that drives our artistic gifts, reflects the power of the unconscious knowledge of The Magician.

The Hero's journey is an act of will now, a calling down of the elements of power available within each of us to step forward into the lab of life. The Magician card is represented by Hermes, Mercury, the malleable, changeable, and elusive chemical. Mercury admonishes us to make the world beautiful, make heaven here on earth. Mercury is the messenger God, god of travelers, alchemists, storytellers, and magicians. In some card depictions the Magician wears an ourobouros belt, the never-ending circle of the serpent swallowing its own tail, or is seen with an infinity symbol over his head. These symbols are sometimes linked to Christ consciousness, the ability to transcend. The card shows us representatives of the four elements: earth, air, fire, and water, plus a fifth: spirit. The Magician says: "Will you?" *You have the power, do you have the will to make magic with it?* We want to add consciousness and will to the impulsive joy of The Fool. There is a hint of the gambler, of taking chances. We must risk the first steps in order to create. The emphasis of the card is on working within the world. We want to draw creativity from within and mix it with the rich elements of the universe to produce gold, to produce *Grace*.

The Fool's staff now becomes The Magician's magic wand. His rucksack of belongings is now filled with his magical tools, those tools representing all possibilities available to the Hero. The Magician is about timing, communication. It is important to pick our field of play, the appropriate tools of communication, so that we do not sabotage our journey. In some Magician cards, we see the symbol of the third eye, the Egyptian Eye of Horus, reminding us to follow our clairvoyant knowing, our inspired communication. In this card we are reminded of the advice of Buddha to combine right speech with right action. We cannot avoid the active forward momentum of Mercury, the planet of communication whose influence is felt in this card. The Fool was an aimless wanderer by comparison. We are now asked to take thoughtful first steps, to draw down the power from within and move toward destiny with all of the creative force of will and inspiration at hand.

The Jungian Saboteur

What holds us back? Fear of failure, of ridicule? Fear that we do not know our way, or do not have the tools we need to complete the task? The Saboteur is the nasty little inner voice that predicts failure by our own hands, right? It's not an exterior force that will get us, it's our own self-doubting. If something is going to go wrong, generally we are the first ones on the scene. We did it to ourselves. Perhaps this is what makes us mortal, not gods. But if anything is going to derail our Hummingbird journey it is our own lack of courage. You have the strength of the Archetypes within you now and there is no place for the saboteur in your consciousness. If you are having doubts, we must unpack them down to their source. Is there a flaw in the plan? Is there an unnecessary detour on the path that has cropped up to bring you up short? When you think about your destiny, are you filled with joy and grace, or does your gut clench and your mind fill with chatter about all the obstacles and ingredients for failure that crowd around you? We all know the feeling. How many times have you said to a friend, "I have the greatest idea!" But as you proceed to explain it you find yourself adding caveats and diminishing the importance of the work or your role in it, until the conversation finds an awkward stall with that common phrase, "Well, it seemed like a good idea at the time." What is the shadow Saboteur doing to us? To some degree, we all need to run through checks and balances before we open our mouths with the words. No, we can't run away from home and survive by our wits. All of our logical faculties must be in play with our dreaming, but they don't have to undermine our work, predetermine failure.

The journey of Hummingbird is an adventure that includes challenges of will and of grace. That's part of the gift. As we move along the path, we expand with joy and with grace. At every turn, we are given another opportunity to taste the nectar, to grow and to nourish. We have no need of the saboteur if we take each step of the journey as a gift to enlarge our deepest self.

Exercise:

Once again, we want to draw our own version of The Magician tarot card. This is you as Alchemist, as Magician. What do you see? What does your magic wand look like and what powers does it hold? What is in your magic tool kit? What is essential for your journey?

The Magician Altar: The Alchemy of the Sacred

Your altar should reflect the universal elements required for the journey: Earth, Air, Fire, Water, and Spirit. We must understand and honor the core connectedness of all things. As you prepare for this meditation, step into the role of Magician. What is your dress? Make this a permanent costume, your regalia, equipage: the tools that you wear. You will want to step into the role of Magician over and over again on your journey. Make your altar and your ritual dress in such a way that you can have it at hand when you need it. The garments should be significant, and from now on, when you step into them, you will be The Magician, you will step into the sacred and gather the force of your power around you. I always think of the Magician as masculine, the strength of the dagger and sword, of a towering presence. Though many of my examples are feminine, don't be fooled, the most powerful shaman I know are men. They are also often the best shape-shifters. What animal comes into your realm to assist you?

Prepare your altar and dress with ceremonial intent. When you are ready, light your candles and incense and begin your breathing.

The Magician Meditation

You wear the rainbow cloak,
each color is a path of power,
an element of the patterns of life.
Earth, Air, Fire, Water, Spirit:
you have the power to call and combine.

You are the first step
you are the singing that is the world.
Your partner is Mercury, the messenger,
bright swiftness, bringer of light.
Your coat is patched with pockets of stardust,
a magic wand is at your side.
The gold and silver of the alchemist's dreams
cascade above you.
Wrap your power around you and rise up,
rise up with grace and joy and step out
into the world.

You are the Magician,
all elements alive around you,
the spark that comes from your finger
is life, is lightning, is your destiny,
your path.
Knowledge is your power,
hold it with grace.

The Mythology of The Magician

I've talked about alchemy in this chapter. *Alchemy* comes from an Arabic word that today commonly refers to the ancient effort to define and refine the element of gold, but the word has deeper roots in a number of practices. In ancient cultures from Mesopotamia to Asia to Europe, esoteric seekers involved in alchemical investigation combined numerous philosophies with metallurgy, astrology, medicine, and chemistry to explore the unknown world of the elements. Although on the surface alchemists might have been seen as the world's first chemistry professors, there is also the underlying "cover story" that this chemical pursuit gave to those magicians who wished to pursue the occult (the uncovered) and the esoteric (the unknown) without attracting the attention of the religious institutions that ruled their real world lives. Dr. John Dee, astrologer to Queen Elizabeth I, was one of these alchemists. Galileo, Copernicus, even Isaac Newton were all forced by the constraints of religious authorities to take their work underground and join the cadre of the Hermeticist.

The most organized of these seekers called themselves a part of The Hermetic Tradition. Hermeticists are magicians in the truest sense of the word. They seek to bring down the knowledge of the spirit and unite it with the universe and its elements. They work between the stars and the earth. The Hermetic tradition is secretive in self-defense, the name deriving from the same root from which we get the word hermit. In fact, every religious tradition has its alchemists working in secret to explore the mysteries of that tradition, sometimes with the knowledge and approval of the tradition, sometimes not.

We want to be the alchemists of our own destinies. We want to uncover and combine the elements of our journey with those of the global world. The mythological archetype here is Creator. We are the god in charge of our own destiny. The Magician seeks to alchemically unify the forces within and without, to put us not just on the path, but within the world as one. The magician is not the trickster of Native American lore, that image is more conducive to the Saboteur, isn't it? The trickster trips us up just when we begin to accumulate power and knowledge. The Magician understands that power is not for the "I" but for the "we" of the globe. The great poet Taliesin is an example of the consummate Magician. He held the power that created the empire of King Arthur. The Magician as alchemist seeks to unify the elements of the universe into their most perfect and everlasting form.

Numbers

The alchemical world as well as the mythological world are deeply impregnated with numerological significance. From the Greeks to modern Cabbalists, from Pythagoras to today's String Theory physicists, numbers fascinate us, they define our scientific domain and our esoteric world at one and the same time. Even without digging too deeply we can see sequences that come up in mythology again and again. Odd numbers like threes and nines particularly. Often the Hero's trials come in threes. There are three suitors for the princess, three worlds, three choices, three tasks. There are five ages of Celtic myth, five ages of Mayan prophecy, five directions, and five elements in Chinese myth, five colors of the Tibetan mandala, seven sages of Babylon, seven gates Inanna must pass through, nine gods of Egypt, and my personal favorite, the Celtic ninth wave: we must never venture beyond the ninth wave, which is, of course, about as far as one can go and still be in sight of shore. Wise advice!

Mercury in Mythology

Mercury is the Roman name of the winged messenger god and it is in their myths that Mercury is most prevalent, but he is also found at the right hand of the Celtic god Cernunous. Perhaps this is because Caesar called the Celtic god Lugus, or Lugh, Mercury, in that great tradition of co-opting other peoples' pantheon in order to convert the masses. Mercury is the winged messenger. Mercury, or Hermes as he was also known, was primarily a god who helped the dead move to the Upper world. The god Woden was occasionally known as the Germanic version of Mercury but more often as Odin, the Norse messenger god. Hermes, the precursor Greek deity, was the god of travelers and we recognize his image by his winged sandals. Hermes was an adept shape-shifter and had the ability to change others into any form he wished. Mercury's day is Wednesday, the root of the English word being Germanic in honor of Woden.

The Romans named the smallest planet Mercury, and the symbol for the planet is adapted from the symbol for Hermes' caduceus. Astrological significance for Mercury adds an element of swiftness and changeability to the subject at hand. The element of Air is the most elusive of our elements. Mercury rules Virgo and Gemini, both signs of communicators.

Sometimes when we sabotage ourselves the most, it is because we fall under the spell of Mercury. We are changeable, malleable, we are not firm in our convictions and thus we're prey to outside influence as well as to the little doubting voice within. When are you most subject to the negative influence of Mercury? When have you rushed to make a decision that later backfired? Or, when have you delayed making up your mind only to find you have caused circumstances to change irreparably by that delay? On the other hand, we can take advantage of Mercury's influence to speed us on our way, to lend us his winged sandals, and give us the grace of gods, that swift light of wisdom and power we think of as "a great idea."

Exercise:

Our charter as Magician is to find the way in which we can individually contribute to the elemental unification and understanding of the universe. I know people who spend their weekends picking up other people's trash. I know people who collect road kill off the highways and give it respectful disposal. I know people who harbor injured birds until they can be released again, and people who steward the marine life on our ocean beaches. These people have one thing in common: their passionate generosity. They have normal lives, jobs, kids, vacations, favorite TV shows, but they would never drive past a dead deer, or walk by an empty beer can, or leave an injured bird to die a painful death. They know how to act on behalf of their fellow beings. They have an innate awareness that we are all together on this planet, every stone, every plant, every animal, every single person.

What is it that you can bring magic to? What act can you perform with sacred devotion that will benefit us all? Choose something you can do over and over again. This is a choice to act on behalf of all. What aspect of the act will draw from your alchemical skills? Recognize every negative thought that comes to you as your own inner saboteur making excuses. To be on the path is to be of service, to strive to be in balance with the world means being generous without requiring acknowledgment. What will you do?

10

The Lovers

The Card

The Lovers falls in the placement of card 6 in the Major Arcana. It is a card of beginnings, connections, value beyond simple material gain. Love is promise. Love is blind. Love is union, the union of male and female but also of passion and compassion. Passion and Compassion: inner desire and its worldly counterpart. Both words have as their root the late Latin word for suffering. In the word compassion, suffering becomes sympathy because it is our recognition of the state of suffering in someone else. When we think of the word *passion* we conjure up rapid heart rates, exploring the limits of our ability to feel and communicate extremes. But what do you think about when you hear the word *compassion*? Gentleness? Kindness, tolerance, restraint of passion, even? There's an element of something else as well, isn't there? I'm compassionate because *I* know better and I can be forgiving this time, or in the Buddhist way, I am compassionate in the face of provocation because I have attained a higher level of knowledge.

The Lovers tarot card is the first moment in the tarot Hero's journey that he is being asked to turn his self-loving quest outward, he is being advised that love brings compassion, because compassion is a higher goal. Love is out of our control, it is blind, accidental, but it brings us the taste, the opportunity for transformation. Physical love shows us the power inherent in love with a capital L.

The Lovers card often depicts four figures: two women, one man, and cupid. Some later cards show Adam and Eve, an angel/cupid, and a snake. In the cards with two women the question is: will you choose Sensuality or Virtue? In other words, will you remain at the level of your own inward drawn base nature, satisfying sexual desire but not looking for connection, or will you move from passion to compassion? This movement to compassion is the unity of the opposites: of the feminine and the masculine in balance. The male and female together are offered Choice. At last! A chance to be in control of Fate! On the surface, The Lovers implies our heart's desire: love. But the extended opportunity is the integration of our masculine and feminine natures, reunite them in order to have the choice to decide for ourselves how to love. Compassion is the manifestation of that choice.

Astrologically, The Lovers is understandably ruled by Gemini, the twins, the masculine and the feminine. They work together to challenge our decision-making abilities, and rightly so. Decisions about love should not be made lightly. We can also gain from Gemini the insight that there is an inner world and an outer world of love. The indiscriminate nature of Cupid and her effect on our inner, personal world of love shakes us to our core. We can overcome that instability with, the card says, stability, perhaps marriage, with choice. In the outer world manifestation, compassion, the Gemini nature of the card, allows us to be flexible and work in both the feminine and the masculine worlds. The card is about relationship, your personal one and the relationship between you and the universe, and whether you rely on Fate to bring love to your world, or whether you make love a conscious choice.

The Jungian Prostitute

Aristophanes, discoursing in Plato's *Symposium*, tells the story of how man and women were first created. In the beginning, he says, humans were tri-sexual and self contained; the male part came from the Sun, the female came from the Earth, while the third, and completing component, came from the Moon and contained both male and female.

Being so complete these creatures became prideful and challenged the gods authority over them. Zeus, angered by their overreaching behavior, pondered what to do—kill them with lightning, banish them? These options, though tempting to a God so volatile seemed contrary to his purposes. In the end, Zeus decided to sever the human form as it was then into two parts and with some basic body adjustments, tying them off at the navel and moving their genitals into better placement. Zeus was satisfied that he had reduced the human to his proper state. From that time forward, men and women would forever and ultimately be seeking their other half, seeking completion. As a result, Love reigns supreme. There is nothing we would not do for Love, no way to stop ourselves searching for the perfect other half. It is in our DNA to search for it, long for it, abandon our "self" for it.

Along the way, the gods allowed us a Fate, usually known as Cupid, whose capricious intervention can create Love where none was before, no matter what we might do ourselves. (The lifeblood of the romance novel, right?) This idea that we have no control over the very thing we most desire is unsettling, isn't it? Yet it seems to be true. Those of us who have experienced love at first sight can attest to the lightning bolt accidental nature of love. There's something about this emotion that is uncontrollable. You cannot manifest it, you cannot call it forth. It doesn't seem fair, does it? The most important aspect of our human countenance is something that Tinkerbell can sprinkle over us, but we can't manifest out of our own desire. Not romantic love anyway, not the partnering kind of relationship love. But perhaps there is a love we can call up.

Our prostitute shadow archetype wants to trade for love, right? We learned to do this back in elementary school, trying to make and keep friends. I'll give you part of my sandwich if you'll play with me this afternoon. Notice me, mark me as special because of your favor. How far were you willing to go for that childish period of grace? Were you willing to dishonor someone else? Children are vicious at the game of love, perfect little prostitutes tasting power for the first time within the circle of their peers.

As adults, we often find ourselves manifesting the Prostitute archetype within relationships in order to get what we want. Sacrificing one part of ourselves for something we value more highly. Sometimes this is perfectly all right. It's how we determine roles and obligations that make society, whether in the larger frame of community or in our own marriages or relationships, run smoothly. When the Prostitute really runs afoul is when it is all too often a part of survival, literally selling one's body to survive.

Think back to your childhood. Can you think of an instance where you called up your Prostitute in order to gain attention? Can you recall a time where your Prostitute's success depended upon the downfall of one of your peers? This is maybe the only good use of a class reunion. Next time you have a chance to attend, go! Find that person you singled our to suffer, and apologize.

Now think about today. Where in your life do you have absolutely no choice but to act from the basis of Prostitute? Can you feel the link between this archetype and your third chakra? Each time you call upon the shadow Prostitute archetype you diminish your self esteem. You can feel your gut clench, can't you? If you have any choice at all, you should ignore the option, but there are truly times for some of us when there is no choice. Think about the word *self-effacing*. Sometimes in our lives we are required to be self-effacing in order to blend in, to attract positive attention. But when does this word take on the mantle of Prostitute? When in your life have you adopted a self-effacing stance when you didn't really feel that way inside? Deconstruct the word, *self effacing,* do you notice how your definition can go from *modest* or *humble* to erasing one's face?

If The Lovers card is ultimately about relationships, about your relationship to the universe, can you now look at your path and see where you have chosen wisely and where you have faltered? Are there moments when, in retrospect, you have stepped off the path in order to satisfy desire? Or where you might be seen to have been walking the path backwards? Blindfolded? Blinded by Cupid? Where along the path have you fallen into the curse of Narcissus? Another form of love, completely self involved. If you begin to live from the base of loving all things, from compassion, how many compromise agreements that you made from your shadow Prostitute will disintegrate? I'm wondering if Cupid is blindfolded because his grace will not fall upon us until we are no longer searching. Give up the search, live from the core of your heart with compassion to all creatures, all life, all universe, and in the moment of your forgetting, love will come.

Exercise:

Draw your own version of The Lovers tarot card. By now I hope you're really into this, and extending the process to include drawing other important cards for yourself. Place the images of the lovers in a context relevant for you. How will you depict the concept of choice? Of randomness? What does compassion look like?

The Sensual and the Spiritual

We want to be awake, fully awake. Rumi tells us, "Love has come to rule and transform, stay awake, my heart, stay awake." This is the transformative nature of love. Of course, Rumi is talking about the kind of love we are working toward, the love of the greater, of the magnificent, of the universal. The linking into *One* kind of love. When we achieve the ecstatic, we have brought about the union of the sensual and the spiritual. It is a love that brings us to our knees. And it is available to us within the hours of each day of our journey. This is what we mean by tasting the sweet nectar, the gifts brought with life. Each moment of joy that brings you to your knees is the transformation of love. Love is the connective tissue of the universe. If we lose the ability to see it, and to honor it, we lose not only ourselves, but the collective destiny of the global community. This love is altruistic, and because it is given freely it is, in the way of the Wicca, returned to us threefold.

The Lovers' Altar

All of your altar work has been of the most intimate nature, but this altar is perhaps the most reflective of your core. You want to assemble an altar that reflects your transformed self, where compassion reigns supreme. This is the altar where you wear your heart on your sleeve, for all to see and to partake of your compassionate love.

Prepare yourself before your altar with a ritual bath, beginning with your own body. Accept, pamper, preen, love the body you have, and love the fact of your body. Your body makes this journey so much easier. Treat it gently, ease into the bath, luxuriate in it. Banish all negative thoughts. The sensual and the sexual are the first step. Indulge in them here, for, like this time before your meditation, they are only acts preparing the field, furrowing the desire, readying your self for the transformative power of love. Awaken all of your body and mind's sensual and spiritual awareness and feel how alike they are. We can see now why Rumi's poetry is so seductive, so ecstatic. Bridge the gap between body and spirit. Fly.

The Lovers Meditation

You are Aphrodite and Eros,
Cupid and Psyche. Masculine,
and Feminine Divine.
You are Gemini and Venus, star-crossed
and planetary.
Seeker and sought, you are lover and loved:
Beloved. Stay awake.

You are Etain and Ailill,
Gráinne and Diarmuid,
desperate and emboldened by love.
You are Deirdre and Naisi
you are Tristan and Isolde,
star crossed and destined.
You are Cybele and Attis,
Samson and Delilah,
Adam and Eve you are.

Choice is yours. Stay awake, beloved,
transformation is near.
You are passionate fusion,
union divine, all hope and certainty is yours.
It is not who you love,
but that you love,
not how you love, but will you love?

It is the coming of grace
the sweet blanket of compassion
wrap yourself tightly, be generous,
there is room for all.
Stay awake, beloved. Stay awake dear heart,
Stay awake.

The Mythology of The Lovers

Star crossed lovers, pick a pair and read their stories: Arthur and Guinevere, Tristan and Isolde, Romeo and Juliet. Some of them are classic tales told from real lives, others are myths. They all have one primary theme: the lead actors follow their hearts, even to the point of death. It's love. We will do anything for love. Joan of Arc gave her life for the love of her God. Plenty of others would give their lives rather than sacrifice their love. This is the strongest emotional bond we can make.

And then there's Narcissus. What an extraordinary predicament! Echo loves him, and she is blind, she cannot see his beauty, the thing he's famous for. Their curse (have you noticed there's always a curse involved?) is that she can only echo the last word he says. It might make an interesting game to try and formulate a conversation between Narcissus and Echo that actually goes someplace based on that rule. In any case, Narcissus represents the worst, most shallow kind of love, self-love. It makes us squirm, doesn't it? It's movie star time. It's everything we are certain we are not. Let's take a serious look at ourselves and see if we catch a glimpse of Narcissus' shadow lurking in the background, holding us, keeping us from reaching that state of compassion we need to be in on our journey. Where does Narcissus surface for you? Do you see him in the mirror in the classic way of the myth? Or is it more subtle? I confess I see him, just a shadow here and there, creeping into a sentence or two of the writing of this book. I'm a naturally shy person, and often I find myself in a trap between shy person and know-it-all, particularly when I'm with people who don't know me. Misunderstood? Perhaps, or perhaps the vain little shadow in me pushes out. You know that old Victorian novel phrase, "she flatters herself…." This is our Narcissus shadow. When we are more entranced by ourselves than by the world around us. We have to be careful that we don't end right back at the level of Serpent, working out our issues! Narcissus gives us an excuse to avoid connecting. Self-involved people never connect.

In a last assessment of the Prostitute archetype, let's look briefly at Samson and Delilah. I love that the issue here is hair. Isn't hair always the issue?! In Samson's case, we learn about temptation, but also about power: where does your power reside? Samson's is, of course, in his hair.

Is this a euphemism? Who knows, anyway, what are you willing to trade for power on the battlefield of love? Where does your Prostitute step up and say, *I'll give you some of this for some of that power.* Have you noticed how much power and sex are connected in politics? They are the same shadow urge, aren't they? It shouldn't be that hard to rise above the basic urges, but they certainly seem to stop some people and completely push them off their paths. If we allow the Prostitute to trade for bits of our self esteem we only delay moving forward on our journey. In some cases, we terminate the destiny altogether, subvert it completely into a mode of simple survival in which we might survive, but we will never love, be loved, or learn the transformative power of compassion and union.

Exercise: Loving Without an Agenda

Well, now, you'd just like to see me perform this miracle, wouldn't you? It might be easier than you think. You're ready for this now, you know it in your heart. You've done your work, chosen your path, moved along it acquiring tools and methods by which to effect the change required to realize your vision. How is it going?

In your journal head a page with two columns, one titled you, one titled with a name that represents the service project you have chosen.

In column 1 (you) list three "tools" you use daily to remind yourself of your path as Hummingbird.

Then list three "tools" you should use, but don't. If any of these three in the least little bit reflect a shadow archetype, put a "P" for Prostitute next to the word.

In column 2 (act of service) list three "tools" you use daily to effect the work needed.

Then list three "tools" you should source, but haven't yet.

Take an analytical look at your lists. Any "P" words? Why do you think you have had to resort to shadow work to get what you need? Can you eliminate that behavior? Why or why not? Write about this in your journal until you feel you understand the lingering shadow and the work you need to do to dispel it.

Finally, pick one "tool" from Column 2 that you don't yet have available and define a strategy for gaining that source. If you like working in the mandala format, do a sand painting around the status of your path. Where are you now? Where are you going? You are the Hero of your journey. Draw yourself and all those around you. How has compassion made a difference in your feeling of community? When there have been moments of stasis, inertia, voids in your progress, what has held you back? What has helped you move forward? Write these things down so that in the future, when you have slack periods, you will already have keys at hand to help snap you out of your lethargy.

If your analysis didn't produce any shadow archetype behavior, congratulations! Your final meditation work will be much easier for that fact. If you did identify shadow archetypes, work with them. Do the work at the level of the sacred, of ceremony. The level beyond words. We can throw words at problems for a lifetime and not resolve them, but if we give up the story, give it to the level of spirit, of the unspoken, we can sometimes effect miracles.

With these primary tools you are ready to wear your heart on your sleeve. You are ready to love without an agenda, because agendas imply shadows, bargains, deals made at the expense of your heart, your mind, your self esteem. Love with abandon, love knowing that you are on your path and you will only meet those who will love you in return along the way, because you have come to this point in balance. And that is the subject of our next meditation: Justice. Step up and sit on the scales.

11

Justice

Reckoning

When we think about Justice, we probably first think about fairness, about laws, the judicial system under which we live, the code of behavior currently acceptable. But for our work here, we want to think about Justice in terms of balance. The Q'ero use the Quechua word "ayni" meaning "right balance." For them, *ayni* represents a relationship contract and is applied between each person and the other members of their village, as well as each individual and the Pachamama, the Earth. *Ayni* functions as a system of reciprocity within their civic life, often replacing money. Philosophically though, right balance is the spiritual goal for each individual as well. The Q'ero make offerings to the Pachamama before each meal in order to balance their relationship with the earth and the food they have taken from her. In their work, they cooperate in a system of reciprocity in order to survive. You help me harvest corn, and in return I'll help you plant potatoes, and we will all benefit by the bounty produced.

The work we have done over the past ten meditations has moved us along the path toward this moment where we will assess our sense of balance within the world. What was it that we were searching for? What is our grail quest, how does it personally manifest for us? It is the search for perfect right balance. If we are in *ayni*, in perfect right balance, then everything that happens is as it should be. We are never late, never early, never missing out, never getting too much or too little. Whether we succeed or fail, it is as it should be. Our failures lead to some better notion or place than some momentary success might have afforded. It sounds Buddhist doesn't it?

Play a quick game. Think of three examples where you can fill in the blanks of this statement in a positive way. *If I hadn't _____, then I wouldn't have _____.* I'll play too. If I hadn't come home from university unexpectedly, I wouldn't have met the man I married, my one true love. Sometimes, like my unexpected trip home to see my folks, these just moments are life shaping, earth shaking events. Major changes in our lives evolve from these instances. We might think of this as randomness, of chance, but the Q'ero teach us that IF we are in *ayni* these events are synchronous. They happen because we are in balance. They are justice served. Synchronicity implies a connectedness, not random, a perfectness in the relationship between ourselves and the universe. Remember how we started? With The Fool dancing along the edge of a precipice, ignorant of potential danger. Now we can see her as Balancing. Trusting in being in complete accord with her universe. This has always been our goal as well. We want our journey to consist of perfect moments of synchronicity, a journey in which we let go of conscious control. Remember when we talked about *karma* and *dharma*? We want to dispense with the give and take of karmic law. We want to live in the moment in balance. That's dharma. And if we are in that moment in right balance with ourselves and the world around us, then we are exactly where we belong at all times, acting within the grace of *ayni*.

You have worked hard over the last ten meditations to explore your own potential and define your own path. If you have been successful you can probably identify moments of synchronicity that have begun to occur more and more frequently as you progressed along your Hero's path. Perhaps just when you figured out what your act of service should be you ran into the very person who could move you forward on that particular journey. Or you began to notice that the media was full of references to people successfully doing the same sort of work you have chosen to do, your tribe of peers, your connections. Even small instances of synchronicity can be immensely validating when we are stepping out on our path. When I came home from my first shaman class I was excited to gather together my medicine bundle, we call them *mesas*. I identify strongly with the owl totem and I wanted to find owl feathers. I remembered meeting a woman I have mentioned before, her act of service is to run a sanctuary for injured raptors. I was wandering around the grocery store in a sort of daze shortly after my return from class, thinking about her, wondering how she was….and then, there she was, right around the next corner! I hadn't seen her in nearly ten years. We talked and she arranged to give me owl feathers for my mesa. But you do this all the time as well, don't you? You're just thinking about someone and the phone rings and there they are. You need something and the very person who can help you get it walks around the corner of the grocery aisle. These aren't accidents. This is synchronicity. And synchronicity only happens when we are in right balance, in *ayni*.

The Card

The tarot card Justice arrives in position 11 in the Major Arcana spread. Half-way through the deck's Major cycle. From this point onward, our work is at the level of the sacred. Previous cards have dealt with influences: romance, position in the world, the acquisition of tools of understanding. But when we have obtained this position, we face a reckoning. We approach the scales and pile all of our accumulated knowledge onto one side, and then we sit on the other. What happens? Have we learned enough to move forward and sit with the gods? Have we learned all that we need to find ourselves within the universe? Is it time to take our place at the fire?

I love the Justice card in the Golden Tarot deck by Kat Black. Here we see an archangel surrounded by little fairy angels who struggle to help a woman (!) restore balance. Well, we all knew it takes a woman, right? There's an owl in the picture as well, the symbol of wisdom. Feminine, archangel wisdom as the arbiter of balance. She knows how to balance the scales. And I love the written interpretation in this deck. "Sometimes she (Fate) needs a helping hand. All will get what they deserve." A bit of a dichotomy, right? Either we should leave it to Fate or we should control it? Perhaps a better way to put it is that if we have acted in balance, all will get what they deserve, including ourselves!

As shaman we learn about power and control, and about letting go of control. There are places of power called *huacas*, sacred places where you can go to participate in the energy of power. Stonehenge and Machu Picchu are *huacas. Huacas* are energy places, not energy sources, a fine but important distinction. These sacred power spots are the great balancers; *huacas* affect balance and harmony no matter what your personal desired outcome might be. Think about whether you are confident enough in your state of balance to allow a sacred power place to work you over. It's not what you want to change, it's what needs to change. It's a scary act, and the results are often a complete surprise! Shaman can create *huacas* in situations that require objective rebalancing, no one's right, things just need to change. For those of us who cannot manage to come into right balance any other way, consulting a shaman might be a good idea. It's important for us to understand that non-control is not chaos. Non-control is asking Spirit to step in where we have failed.

In other decks, the Justice tarot card implies a spiritual awakening, pictured by a veil. Lifting the veil is the dawn of awareness breaking. Where in your life do you see this awareness happening for you? How is it changing your ability to interact with others? Are you sometimes feeling a little apart from your peers? It does take some adjusting, this being in dharma sensibility.

Justice is about truth and right judgment. Justice is associated astrologically with the sign of Libra. Libra's traditional symbol is the scales. In the Renaissance deck, Justice is represented by the goddess Athena, and the sacred owl is traditionally her familiar. Athena is the goddess of rational thought, defender of just causes. In interpreting this card, there is again an element of everyone getting what they deserve. This is sort of a backhanded version of *ayni.*

Justice is always depicted as a woman. Often in her hand is a sword, the sword or staff of authority. Athena mythology is strong feminine power although not generally very rational, but then we don't often see rational behavior from the gods. You'll learn more about her later in this chapter. Athena is wise, like the owl who represents her, and in her mythology we might call her thoughtful more than rational, for she was very good at clever ways to get what she wanted.

The Jungian Victim

Victim, the fourth and last Jungian archetype, takes us back to our third chakra work, doesn't it? We fall into victim when we compromise our self, our ego, our instinct. Early on in our evolution, it may have been convenient to rely on our shadow Victim in order to avoid facing up to certain truths about ourselves. Victim archetype behavior is all about excuse-hood. I can't do *this* because I was *that*. Fill in the blank for yourself. Do you also see that this is diametrically opposed to our examples of synchronicity?

All of the enormous catalog of ills, hurts, abuses that we can each of us list are potentials for us to act from Victim. And sometimes, we just can't muscle our way beyond it, sometimes we are doomed to carry the history of victimhood with us, even from past lives. This historical embedded Victim often will require outside intervention to truly shed, this is the work of a shaman. But at this point in your work, you should cringe when the temptation to draw on Victim behavior arises. Every time the opportunity arises to step back from being wholly on your path because it's risky, or scary, or a wee bit challenging, there will be a tidy list of excuses ready at hand for you to choose from, but don't. *Because every time you step into Victim, you step completely off your path.* It's like monopoly and you've just been sent to jail. When we can accomplish releasing Victim in favor of Justice, of right balance, then we are ready for the Hero's final journey, the ascent to the mystical goal, to the sacred. Most of the behavior that gets us into the greatest trouble comes from acting on our Victim archetype. As a world, this is also true. Countries do this all the time.

We generally associate Victim with women, don't we? Why is that? It's because it's weak behavior, behavior without responsibility. But our subconscious doesn't differentiate. Men are perhaps quieter about their Victim shadows but they are just as powerfully controlled by them, and more dangerous. What wars have been started by men acting from Victim?

The Justice card reminds us that all things are interconnected. Some cards even depict a spider and her web. Nothing is decided or effected in a vacuum. The Druid Craft Tarot tells us that the scales represent "the perfect moment of the Present, balanced between Past and Future." The card rests in the exact middle of the 21 card progression. The Justice card asks us to be aware of which of our acts are reactions and which are actions and how these two different modes create ripples of consequence through our lives, and thus impact our journey.

Exercise: Draw the new card.

The old card shows an owl, a sword, and a magnificently powerful woman. Can you top that? What elements do you personally need to see on the card of right balance? Are you ready for the figure on the card, whether you are male or female, to be you?

The Justice Altar

So much of the point of this meditation is mental attitude adjustment. The Justice card is represented by the element Air. You can tell, can't you? Let's create an altar that represents your perfect present. What perfect thing symbolizes you at this moment on your path? Perhaps a small animal fetish, photo, a particular flower or herb, self portrait or piece of clothing, a feather. Put this on the right hand side of your altar space. On the left pile symbols of all of the most important things you have tried to be or do or wished. In the center, place a symbol of the focus of your current journey, that thing or act that you have decided to devote yourself to. Cover the whole altar with a thin veil, a sheer scarf or piece of voile.

As you work with this altar, notice how the veil separates you from your identities in a way that allows you a different perspective. Spend some time with your journal writing about each element that you placed on the left side of your altar. Which elements are still valuable? Which are not? You may find that during the course of this month you dismantle bits of the left side, discarding things that no longer serve. To move forward on the Hero's path, from this point onward, we need to be clean, completely clear of attachments that tether us to the Victim archetype. If you honestly cannot let go of one or two attachments, try to follow their thread back to the source. Which chakra is holding that wound? Try involving the archetype governing that chakra. If the issue is sexual, for example, ask Jaguar to intervene. Acknowledge that you've done the work in your head without success and give it over to the power of the sacred, to Jaguar. We don't have to work out every problem in thought and words. In fact, it's much more effective to allow the work to be done at the higher non-verbal, sacred level. This is the universal consciousness that Jung talked about. The realm of archetypal behavior in which we all share. Jung might have preferred to call it super-conscious, or unconscious, while we will call it mythic or sacred. Let any residual problems be worked out at the mythic.

Work with your altar until you are satisfied that everything represented there is essential, *essential,* to your present path. Take as long as you need for this process, and notice that much of the work will happen while you are doing other things. You'll work with your altar and then go on about your ordinary day, and then you'll walk by and notice something there, and say, wow, why is *that* still there, I don't need that!

When you are satisfied that your altar represents your essential self, remove the veil and prepare for the Justice meditation.

The Justice Meditation

There is an island distant from you,
a veil of cloud and mist and
fog obscures your view,
but there in the distance
you can faintly see a figure,
a woman dressed in the reflection of the sea.
She is an archangel, a goddess, Athena, is she.
Tiny angels tie her sandals
and carry her long robes behind her.
An owl stands by her side.
In her right hand she holds the golden scales of
truth,
in her left the sword of right judgment.

She is Athena, triple born,
sprung from the head of Zeus,
virgin goddess of wisdom, the defender.
Are you ready to come before her?
Are you ready to lay all of the acts
of this life upon
the scales of her just conviction?

She is Justice, She is Athene, the spider is she,
creator of the web of connection that binds
your world.
Where are you in the tangle that is creation?
How are you attached to the world?
Who do you touch? Who touches you?

If all life is a cycle, where is your beginning
and your end?
Where do you falter? Where do you soar?
If the wise Owl had one word or phrase for you

What would it be?
Would it be Act? Stay awake? Pray? Live?
Would it be Love? Give? Believe?
Where does your wisdom lie?

Imagine the Owl
speaking those wise words to you,
take the words in your prayer pose hands and
hold them before you, breathe into the words,
give your oath to these words, three times three
for it is to yourself that you promise
a wise one's journey to be.

The Mythology of Justice

Athena, or Athene as she is sometimes written, is the Greek goddess born from the head of Zeus. Like Ishtar, Atargates, Neith, Persephone, and Arachne she is associated with the spider as a weaver of destiny, and so she is the perfect completion to our eleven meditations. Most of the mythology of Athena speaks of her strength and power, not of her as a particularly outstanding proponent of justice (not many of the gods were just, as my Classics professor friend will tell you). Athena was a fighter and could be dreadfully jealous. She was a virgin and had been born from the forehead of Zeus after Zeus swallowed her mother, Metis, in order to prevent her bearing his child. Homer tells us that Athena was known as *glaukos*, gleaming because of her hazel blue eyed steady gaze. This word is the same as the root for owl, her familiar. The piercing gaze of the just and wise. She is associated with the number three as the third daughter of Zeus. Athena may be a morphing of the Egyptian goddess Neith, also a spider goddess, and both are patron goddesses of weaving. It was Athena who turned the weaver Arachne into a spider when she dared to anger Athena by declaring herself the superior weaver. Athena is rather more identified with war, strength, and wisdom than she is with justice except for one very important episode in her mythology.

Where Athena rises to the status of Justice is when we find that she is credited with establishing the first human jury. In a particularly unfortunate tale, a family generational curse persistently resists being avoided. The story is about the house of Atreus, who for shallow reasons began killing and eating various family members. Try as they might, the subsequent generations of the family found themselves repeating the curse. It wasn't until many generations later, one distraught family member sought the judgment of Athena, that the curse was broken. Athena, in clearing the curse, assembled the first jury of peers, of humans. Prior to that, all decisions were made by the gods. The story of the generational curse and how unavoidable it was shows us a parable about how easy it is to remain in the clutches of the Victim archetype. He did that to me, so I'm going to steadfastly refuse to learn from this curse and instead I'm going to do the same thing to the next person who will let me get away with the act. We see this all the time in child abuse, spousal abuse situations don't we? But it also sort of sums up all of baser human behavior. The Perpetrator-Victim-

Enabler cycle. What is it about Victim that makes the line between Victim and Perpetrator so thin and so very easy to cross? What is it about human logic that makes the cycle so easy to manifest?

In order to progress into the realm of the sacred, to move forward on your path clear of the negative cycles of the Victim archetype, you have a rather heavy load of past behavior to shed. You've done this, beginning with the Serpent archetype and the most primitive sense of self. What should be left for you is only the memory, the history, though you should acknowledge the residual power that even memory has over you. There is residual power in past life "unremembered" history, as well. You should feel as though you have done all the work you can. Now I want you to take what is left, your remembered and unremembered history, and step into the sacred. By stepping into the sacred, you complete your circle, you return to the collective unconscious all of the archetypal baggage, you give up control and rely upon your connectedness to the collective. The path becomes destiny, the destiny is sacred work, "we" replaces "I" and you move freely about the universe in exquisite balance.

Exercise: Breathing As One

Throughout these eleven meditations, we have used breath exercises as the initial "kick start" preparation to our meditative state. Breath work is a powerful tool. When you are with other people, in casual conversation, during disagreements, notice your breathing, and notice their breathing. How do they compare? If you're a parent and you are lecturing your child, what is your breath like, and what is theirs? Try to match your breathing to someone else. Notice during lovemaking that your breathing matches. Notice also how hard it is to fight with someone once you match your breathing to theirs.

If we are to move along our path synchronously, we need to be in sync with each other physically. We can do this by matching our breathing. Notice sighs, exhales of contentment or of dismay. Watch your own breathing responses. Do you have a habit of breathing shallowly? Learn to breathe deeply of the mother, her air is your life blood, breathing shallowly is an indication of not being very grounded or committed. Take advantage of your physical body. Commit yourself to the earth, breathe her in, breathe her out, breathe as one.

12

The Twelfth Night

The Search for Self

There is a Northwest Coast myth sometimes called *Skeleton Woman*. This Inuit story beautifully recounted by Clarissa Pinkola Estes in *Women Who Run With The Wolves*, explains to us the interconnectedness of the life/death cycle. The young woman in the story dies a violent death and her body is stripped down to its bones by the creatures of the ocean floor until over time, nothing remains but her skeleton. A fisherman catches her on his line and through his own misfortune and panic he drags her home, her bones a tangle of broken pieces. As his panic recedes, the fisherman finds within himself a seed of empathy for the skeleton, and so he untangles her from his fishing line and realigns her bones this way and that until they once again form the basis of a body. By the firelight, the fisherman falls asleep, and in his sleep he sheds a single tear. The Skeleton Woman sees the tear, and in her hunger and thirst she moves over the fisherman and drinks the tear from his cheek. And so she begins to reform her body, adding flesh and organs, eyes and hair, until she is fully a woman again, whereupon she lies down beside the fisherman and joins with him, in life.

What we have tried to do in the past eleven meditations is strip down to the bones of our essential self. We have cast aside the impediments of shadow archetypes, recognizing them as barriers to accessing our destiny. At this point in your work, the temptation to fall into shadow behavior should bring a jarring moment of discontinuity to you. Shadow archetype behavior in those around you should make you cringe. We have spent eleven months working on our bare bone self. Our skeleton. And like Skeleton Woman we are now ready to accept that single tear, that single momentary gift of life, of rebirth, of destiny. What is it that the single tear signifies for you? What is the single moment of awakening that will give you the motivation to re-flesh, revive, rebirth? Clarissa Pinkola Estes talks about the difference between loving self, and loving others. Of creating through tears. We want also to love our destiny, love the journey, each step of the path before us.

The Muse Within The Earth

What if the tear that falls from the fisherman's eye is the gift of life itself? And what if that gift of life is the spark, the regenerative creative voice that rises up in each of us and declares the dawn of a new and exciting day? Where does this muse come from? She comes from the earth and our connectedness within the web that is our existence, our destiny. What is a web without a weaver? Chaos. We look around ourselves in nature and find proof everywhere we look that chaos does not reign. We find proof everywhere we look that there is order and connectedness to a degree that we in our small existence are only minutely aware. The teardrop of life, of being sustained, is the creative force that refuses to let go, that understands that life and death are cycles, not linear goalposts, but a beautiful web.

The work you have done in the past meditations has drawn a diagram of your own personal web, fleshed out its skeletal image with personal goals, with people who are dear to you, with events that have shaped your life. This web is like a snowflake, the pattern of it is uniquely your own. The mythology that impacts your personal process is yours, assembled from your own personal archetypal choices. Now that we have empowered your chakras, now that we have dispelled your shadows, you are ready to define your destiny, access your power archetype, and move into the Hero's journey confident that you are exactly where you belong, doing exactly what you should be doing.

We have worked with, and dispelled, the curse of shadow archetypes. But we all have archetypal longings. We can all identify certain attractive patterns that mold or guide us in our behavior in this body, this lifetime. It's important to identify and recognize these archetypes. Who is King? Who is the Student, Who is the Nun, who is the Caregiver? If you have worked through Caroline Myss's *Sacred Contracts*, you have the answer to this at hand. If you haven't, then spend some time listing six or eight primary archetypes that describe you. I would choose Queen, Scholar, Poet, Hermit, Friend, and Lover. What would you choose? Don't worry about the fact that all archetypes have a shadow side, the evil twin that can be provoked. Just think about your callings. Who are you? Narrow the list down to the two or three most important archetypes that guide you, and write down some adjectives that described that archetype.

The Card

Take a tarot deck of your choice and spread out the twenty-two Major Arcana cards in any order. Look at the images on the cards, don't worry about reading the divinatory meanings quite yet. Take your time and examine all the cards one at a time. If you come across cards that seem to resonate with you, speak to you, set them aside. Then, from that group of meaningful cards, pick the three that resonate the most. The three cards you feel compelled to pick. Lay them out before you.

Which card did you put in the first position? Why do you think the card has meaning for you? What about the second? And then the third? Now that you have looked at the three cards, does it seem like there is an order to them? Are they in the correct order? If you were to look at the cards as representing the past, the present and the future, would you shift their positions? If so, realign them now.

Let's look at the cards as if the first card is your past. Do you have a sense of "been there, done that?" Good. Put that card back in the deck. Lessons learned. If not, why not? Is there something there you want to hang on to? Something you feel you absolutely must carry with you? Are you sure? If you have to keep the card, leave it in its position for now. Look at the card in the middle, the present, and ask yourself how you feel looking at the card? What if, for example, you chose The Tower?

That card depicts a castle coming to fire and ruin, people are falling out of the top stories of the tower. Destruction seems to reign. If I chose that card and it lands in this position, I would think that utter and complete change was occurring in my life now. Maybe even destructive change. The tearing down of the physical reality of my world. If the card you have chosen in this position makes sense to you, and you accept it, leave it aside. Now look at the third card, the future, and create the story, the mythology that you see in the card. Is this your destiny? Is this card accurately showing your path? If not, is it showing obstacles, difficulties, shadows? Why do you think you picked this card? Are there areas in your shadow work that are not completed? Are you blocking your ability to step fully onto your path, or is someone or something else making obstacles in your way? At this point if you need further elaboration, you can read the divinatory meanings, but keep in mind that what you conjure in your head actually counts for more right now than the written meanings. We are working at the level of myth, beyond words, we are working at the level of sacred images.

Of the three cards, which one really resonates as the "that's me, oh yes!" card? All during the writing of this book, my card, the one I keep picking intentionally or otherwise has been The Fool. If you have been working with the cards while we've been progressing through the meditations, you will probably have noticed that you keep picking the same card or cards. It's funny how the same issues come up for us again and again! By the same token, (and isn't that an interesting phrase) the card that speaks to us, is our symbolic destiny. The Fool, stepping blissfully off into the future, or off the path of what is generally accepted as "normal"—yep, that's my card!

Exercise:

The New Card—Draw your new card, combining the elements of the three cards you chose from the Major Arcana and incorporating three key elements of your destiny with symbols for each. Use the descriptions of the personal archetypes that you chose for yourself to help create this new power archetype.

The Twelfth Night Altar

In fleshing out your own skeleton you have accumulated personal power objects and symbols that you should now easily be able to assemble into this final altar. Along the way have you acquired a hummingbird? Prepare your altar with every bit of ceremony you can conjure. This is your ultimate personal ceremony. Celebrate your sensuality, your creativity, your connection to the earth, to the stars, to the creatures of your universe. Celebrate your talent, your glorious body, your generous heart. This might be the altar that takes you some time to lovingly create, the perfect weekend devotion. Don't rush. Take a side trip to visit a labyrinth and walk the meditation course praying about your destiny, your personal Hummingbird journey. Find a symbolic token of your arrival at this moment of understanding, a stone or a charm to carry with you. Bless it and consecrate it on your altar. Know that in doing this work you have arrived in the universe fully prepared to work at the level of the sacred.

Once your altar is prepared, sit before it and compose your meditation.

Making Objects Sacred

Talisman. The word is from the Greek for religious rite of payment, but now is taken to mean amulet, a symbolic token meant to protect or confer sacred or magical powers to its wearer. Charm, also a trinket worn to effect particular magic. How do charms get their charm? You can make your own magic, of course. It's all a matter of intent, we know that now, right? However, if you want a classical traditional process, try this: leave the object outside under unobscured moonlight, preferably the full moon over night. To cleanse an object, leave it in sea salt, wash it in the ocean or in pure water in the moonlight. Never wear a charm that you haven't cleansed and made your own with ceremony.

The Twelfth Night Meditation

Many of you are way ahead of me on this, have written your meditation out without prompts or clues, it will have flowed naturally out of the previous work you have done. However, if you panic at the idea of putting together your own mantra, your own poetic lines, here is a simple format for you to use in creating this powerful and very personal meditation.

To begin, think of the purpose of the meditation process. This one is about your destiny, yours alone. Since you are invoking it, it makes sense for the meditation to be in your voice. "*I*_____." Let's take a page or two from the witches' spell casting process and use the number three. Divide your meditation into three parts; within each part have repetitions of threes. Make the first part, the first stanza, declarative:

I am _____. You want to describe your power archetype here. Three ways, three times. Make your sentences as full of evocative words as you can. "I am powerful" is great news, but rather a flat statement isn't it? "I am the power of the mountain waterfall" brings another image to mind entirely, doesn't it?

The second part of the stanza is your declaration of ability. *I can* _____. Again, you are assembling a collection of three statements, three ways. Pull out all the stops! This is your chance to reign.

The final stanza, just like the previous two, will be a series of three statements turned three ways, of intent, "*I will*_____!" Describe your destiny.

End with a single line, a common poetic element to summarize your power into one phrase, one sentence that you can take from the entire meditation as your power mantra. "*I am* _____." This is you, this is what you will repeat under your breath every time life takes a hard turn. Make it work for you, make it ring in your ears. It's a shout from the mountaintop, a call in the darkest cave. Make it roll and boil with power, your power. Three power words that are you from now on.

Ready? Good. Get your journal and write your personal power archetype meditation or write it in the page provided here. Prepare for the meditation as you always do, with bathing, incense, and breathing. Recording your meditation is a great idea, then you can play it back with your eyes closed, or recite along with yourself for double the effect. Work your meditation now.

The Mythology of the Twelfth Night

Now is the fun part: imagining your own myths. First, do a little research. When you looked at the tarot cards, what memories did the images bring back to you? Lately, I keep thinking about Rapunzel. You know, maybe she was up there in the tower writing a book; did anyone ever consider that? Maybe she wasn't lonely, she was just busy! And then there's this big bad wolf who isn't really so bad at all, kind of a pussy cat actually, who keeps sending me e-mail to bolster my spirits, and ravens courting in the oak trees outside my window. All of these are ethereal links to a mythological world that works in my subconscious. We all operate on three levels all at the same time, conscious, subconscious, and super-conscious; what we want to do when we create our own mythology is open the door to our subconscious and let some of those creatures out to play. What stories are at work in your mind? If you were to amend your personal meditation with images from classical or native indigenous mythology what characters would surface? What story can you tell as a morality tale that ends with you stepping onto your path, fully aware? Your myth might begin, "Once upon a time I was_____, but then _____." During the work of the past year, you have acquired totem animals, archangels, spirit guides, and an affinity for myths and legends that rang true for you. How can you incorporate these into your meditation today? And beyond that, how can you take all of these elements forward with you in effecting your destiny?

Exercise: Be As Thou Art

By coming to this point, you have become Hummingbird. You know the sweetness of the journey. You have defined your destiny and made the necessary changes to your life, awareness, and core self in order to realize your goals. The Hero's journey has begun. Take this time to review, but also to make forward progress on the path. Where is your grace? How are you now a generous inclusive being? What have been the moments of synchronicity that have proven to you that this path is your true destiny? Where is the forward momentum?

I hope that you have a sense of the energy and excitement that comes with love, with loving, and being in love, with connecting in the eternal web that is our universal place. The Q'ero have a word in Quechua, *munay*, that simply translated means "love" but in the way of languages where words have many discreet meanings, *munay* with the added *ki*, *munay ki*, may be translated as "be as thou art." The circle of love and loving produces loved and beloved. *Be as thou art.* It's a huge request, but it's the only thing left to us. It's a prayer, a command, a responsibility, a mantra, it is our path.

Part Three

Beyond Meditation

Tarot and the Archetypes

Is This Deck Stacked? Using Tarot to Understand the Journey

All of us, to one degree or another, are stuck in a series of looping behaviors, partly because that's just the way life is, it's not a mathematically satisfactory track of linear experience, and partly because we are adaptive beings who learn by doing, or sometimes we don't learn at all. One of my psychic friends likes to call the transcendence of these loops or patterns "growth periods" and they can be painful, scary times. It's useful to track our patterns; it helps us recognize our resistances. Tarot is one effective way to do this tracking.

Angeles Arrien in *The Tarot Handbook* suggests a daily tarot reading of three cards, each card corresponding basically to sense of self, decision-making trust, and health. Keeping a simple journal entry of the daily cards very quickly begins to reveal patterns. No, the deck isn't stacked; it's ourselves who are stacked, layered with the patterns that hold us back. These are the easy behaviors that allow us to function at a comfortable level, but that do not move us forward on our journey. Arrien's method is to fan the shuffled cards out as if they were your body, one end the head, one the feet, and pull the cards from where you feel strongest—in health, in trust, in self. Even the act of deciding where your strength is for that one day is revealing to us. In deciding where we feel good, we obviously notice where we feel weakest. If you consistently feel your sense of self is in your head but notice that your heart feels torn or your gut feels turbulent, this is information about what impedes your positive forward progress. The tarot card then becomes an expanded clue to the identifying process itself. Your sense of trust in decision-making comes from your gut but your logical mind fights with every gut decision you make; what does this say about you and your journey? Perhaps the tarot card you draw at this point is often the Knight of Swords. The Knight of Swords is the "brash young man, headstrong but with great enthusiasm." This is an interesting way to live, always being the risk-taker. You would want to ask yourself if this approach is working or is it exhausting.

When we draw three cards a day over a period of months, we see patterns develop. There are cards in the seventy-eight card deck that I have never pulled, and there are cards that come up for me week after week after week. Hello! Tarot serves not as a true divination tool but as a fleshing out service for our psyche. It is predicting the future by pointing out where you're stuck in the present. You can use the daily spread pattern from *The Tarot Handbook* (see the bibliography for details) or you can make up your own system, as long as you keep track of the cards pulled over a span of months so that you can see the patterns developing.

Expanded Practice: Exercise, Destiny Draw

Using the whole deck and reading the meanings from the lexicon, pull three cards in the way mentioned above and read the corresponding meanings. Next, return to the spread out deck and let your hand roam up and down over the fan of cards. Take your time, and pull three cards that seem to attract your attention. These are your Shift cards. Notice the way the original three indicate those "stuck" areas of your life path while the new three reflect the optimum pattern of behavior required to move forward. They might even be clues as to the exact changes needed, perhaps the card is one of healthy lifestyle choices, or celebrating family and friends, or even leaving a relationship behind! If you don't take heed of the Shift cards' wisdom, you'll repeat those stuck cards.

If you do not bring forth what is within you, what you do not bring forth will destroy you. –Gospel of St. Thomas

Another way to use the tarot is as a storytelling mechanism. Somewhat akin to the exercise we did earlier in this chapter, lay out only the Major Arcana tarot cards face down and then pull three cards. Write or tell a story using the pictures on the three cards as your plot triggers. First, write a story about a fictional fairytale character. Then write the story again using the same three cards, but with yourself as the main character. It was much harder to write your own story, wasn't it? Where in the story did you get stuck or not want to write the truth? Of the three trigger cards, which one made you stop and think or balk at the plot line that came to you? Turn all of the remaining Major Arcana cards over and choose one card for your "destiny" card, one card to represent who/where you would like to be? What archetype best tells your optimal story? Spend some time reading about the Major Arcana cards and their relation to archetypal myth, and then rewrite your story with the most positive "spin" you can create and still remain true to your life so far. (Banzhaf's *Tarot and the Journey of the Hero* is a great source book for this work.) You should come away from this exercise with motivation and enthusiasm, even if the path so far has been a difficult one; it is the future that counts now.

Sympathetic Magic

This new notion of Creative Visualization is really an age-old witches' trick called Sympathetic Magic. It's easy. The basis of the process is to draw what it is you want to have happen. Drawing it makes it real. How must you change in order to align yourself more perfectly with the universe? Make a detailed drawing of the change, not the problem, the change, the solution. If you draw the problem, you'll stick yourself right inside it and that will be the active center of your story. Draw the solution, use as much detail as you possibly can, spend time on it, invest in it. Post the drawing on your mirror (a common witches' trick), your altar, or some other conspicuous place of honor. Watch the magic happen.

Working with Children

We all wish we could follow Peter Pan right from the start as young children, have the best possible life without the hard work and disappointment. We would like to spare our children from the lessons we learned the hard way. Children have the advantage of an unencumbered imagination and an active, unrepressed sixth sense. Simply encouraging and nurturing these gifts will help them find their path in the most expansive and creative way possible for them. My favorite exercise to do with children is creating spells. Kids love to rhyme, and they love the grisly stuff of witches' cauldrons. Spells are often written in a rather mesmerizing poetic meter called trochaic, from the Greek word *trochos* meaning "wheel." "Double, double toil and trouble" is written in trochaic meter, it has a forward momentum that is rather hypnotic. Now, of course, we don't want to teach children to be making spells out of hand just to create havoc, but it's very nice to make a spell of protection for oneself. Here's the rest of Shakespeare's famous spell:

> Eye of newt and toe of frog,
> wool of bat and tongue of dog,
> Adder's fork, and blindworm's sting,
> Lizard's leg, and howler's wing—
> For a charm of pow'rful trouble,
> Like a hell-broth boil and bubble.
> Double, double toil and trouble.
> Fire burn and cauldron bubble.

Well, the kids would love the squeamish parts, but let's replace the scary bits with some protective insights and some joy. Have the children rhyme some juicy protection and charm themselves with the energy of a simple spell. Here's a spell I wrote:

> Egg and apple, moon and breast
> perfect spiral, circles best
> spinners waulkers fullers friends
> gather now we'll make amends.

Circle dancing take my hand
pass me deosil 'round the land
lifting voices, breasts unfurled
dancing, dancing ribbons curl.

Acorn, hawthorn wort and berry
forgive, forget, forefend. Make merry!

Exercise: What's in the Bag?

Keeping our intuitive power elastic is something we all should practice, but this exercise is especially fun with kids. Get three or four paper sandwich bags and put one random object in each bag—don't show anyone, and don't tell anyone anything about what you put in the bag. Keep the bags hidden.

Have the children sit quietly and focus on their breathing, settling down into themselves just a bit. This would be the perfect time for a short children's yoga session! Once they are a little quiet, bring out one of the paper bags and set it in front of them so that they can all see it, but can't touch it. Have them look at the bag and guess what's inside. Ask them, "What color is it? What shape is it? Is it soft? Hard? Fluffy? Round?" Can they guess what it is? Be quick, don't linger over discussions. Like test taking, one's first impressions are usually correct. This practice will help with test taking later on at school. As the kids try to intuit what's in the bag, some of them will be much better at this than others, but they all can learn to track objects in this way, and later on when they are young adults it will help them keep their personal possessions from being lost! Tracking exercises like this one hone children's attention skills. It isn't so much whether they guess the object as it is their ability to use all of their senses to link their instinctual qualities together to make them active beings. Be sure to point out that it doesn't really matter whether they guessed right or not, but to think about why they guessed the attributes that they did. They are connecting to their unconscious, a powerful source of information, especially when sitting down to take a formula test!

Children and Tarot

Children love tarot cards and don't need any interpretive book to understand the picture on the card. Even children as young as three can draw a card and tell you a fine story about what's going on, both on the card and in their own psyches. What they see as the most important part of the card is sometimes quite astonishing! I guarantee they will see something that you did not. Working with children in the neutral ground of the tarot can ease hidden tension and bring the child out of himself in a way that opens the opportunity to transcend some developing negative behavior. It's usually best to use one card at a time to develop a story. For young children, only one card is needed. Older children will respond to the developing story with anticipation and increasingly creative narrative. Inviting the children to draw the story they created from the tarot card will allow them to fill out details even further.

Children are also adept at "reading" animals. Sit in the park, at the beach, or in your garden and ask the children to name every animal they see or hear. Being in tune with the other species of our planet is a gift we are born with and lose. If we are to evolve, we must hang on to our sensitive natures, care for all creatures, great and small. Squashing bugs and shooting birds with BB guns needs to be replaced with the gentle touch of the universal mother. Asking our children to be "mother" to all creatures, the creepy crawlies as well as the furry ones, asks them to be stewards of the earth, to know the earth intimately, and in time this will allow them to smoothly find their place on her breast.

Conclusion: Tick Tock

Joseph Campbell pointed out to us in his massive exploration and explanation of myth and how it relates to our personal world, that we are essentially adrift. *Essentially* adrift. If you find all these Greek, Egyptian, and Inkan names baffling and hard to pronounce, you are not alone. Perhaps nothing you read of the mythology contained here resonates with you one little bit. It's no accident that we often use the phrase, "It's all Greek to me!" We've lost our way, we've lost our connection to the mythology that was, for the previous two centuries, the glue that held those previous generations of psyches together. That we've lost our way was Campbell's point. At our very essence, our core, we have been cut off from the archetypal history that brings order to mankind. Moreover, when he exhorts us to "follow your bliss", he is suggesting that in order to be whole, we must have the glue of some sort of mythology. Our first step, then, is to develop the myths that we have lying deep in our subconscious. We need to dig deep to reveal archetypes appropriate to our unprecedented time.

During a recent shamanic session I was talking about a vision I had, and I described a faerie-like being that seemed to appear out of the clouds. "She looked like Tinkerbell," I said, "and, you know, she seemed to be saying, 'Believe'!" And my shaman friend laughed and said, "Well, of course she did." It's been a long time since I thought about Peter Pan, perhaps thirty years, and frankly parts of that story scared me, but there were threads in place, weren't there? Threads that have dangled unused for several decades until I happened to allow one to surface in my semiconscious meditative state and there she was, a tiny bit of my own personal mythology.

"And then, to top it off," I said, tapping on my wrist, "Tick Tock!" And my friend laughed at the look on my face as it slowly dawned on me that that too, was a part of the Peter Pan story.

Tick Tock. It's a critical part of our current world story. We don't have time to wander off the path into a Buddhist sort of escapism and ponder what air is like when it does nothing special at all. That Zen koan was for an earlier, safer age. Whatever you must do to claim a mythology, tether your psyche to a healthy, strong, growing life story for this planet, this universe, do it! The Age of Self Indulgence must be replaced by the Age of Generosity. Generosity of spirit. Be generous with yourself and you will heal. Be generous with your personal world, and you will receive love. Be generous with the Earth, and she will carry you on her belly. If your personal mythology begins with Tinkerbell, well then, welcome, apparently, to my club! I'm sure there are more of us around! We are all mythologically challenged, but we don't have to remain so. The most successful archetypal images to incorporate into your personal mythology are those that already reside in your unconscious storehouse. Like my Tinkerbell, we all carry images that relate directly to emotional reactions like the fear and joy that we were exposed to as children, ripe blank slates onto which were imprinted many archetypes, both on purpose (the little boy who cried wolf, for example) or accidentally, as in the case of the crocodile who reminds Captain Hook of his mortality in Peter Pan. When you meditate and when you dream you will follow these tenuous threads. Sometimes the archetypes arise out of a specific need in the moment. Notice how our Greek Hero, Parsifal, manages to run into exactly the right archetypal assistant at exactly the right time along the way. It's not that he couldn't make it on his own. Perhaps he could manage to battle chaos and come out the other side of life whole; but he doesn't have to: he has archetypes to guide him. So do we. Tinkerbell wants me to believe I can fly. The crocodile wants me to realize time's a wasting. They are luminous motivators. My cheering squad. They *will* show up when I need them as long as I am paying attention. The thread that connects me to them is activated in my unconscious exactly when their wisdom is needed. This is the base of ordered existence, of a path defined, a destiny retrieved. To try to make the Hero's journey without archetypal assistance is to remain at the level of The Fool, to dabble in chaos.

Joseph Campbell says that mythology is the language of the self, a language we have forgotten how to read. I took the time to borrow a copy of *Peter Pan* and began to read it. Not very far into the story I realized what it was that triggered the initial sense that I found the story scary: it was Nana, the dog. I remember as a child being completely overwhelmed with worry over Nana's feelings, so worried that the rest of the story became secondary to the anticipation of a happy ending for Nana. Delight in Tinkerbell, the message of the crocodile, these things did not resonate with the child in me. So how, I now wondered, could I make the story work for me?

Exercise: Discovering Personal Myth

Retell a classic fairy tale that was a favorite of your childhood. To make it simple, first think of the tale, and then who is your favorite character in the tale? Concentrate only on that one character. Find a friend who will listen to you tell a story, we want them just to listen, no interruptions allowed! Begin the story as it always must, "Once upon a time...." and continue to tell the story of your one favorite character, but tell it as you see it happening, tell it your way, change the primary parts of the story—the time period, the setting, describe them. In changing the characteristics of the story you make it your own, you make it more relevant to your personal journey. What happens? How does the story end? *Do not preplan your story.* Tell it completely off the cuff, just let the descriptive words roll out of your mouth. If you want to, stand up in front of your friend and use your body language to dance the story while your words come. Use the graceful traditional native ways of storytelling with arm and hand gestures. If you're shy, have your listener just listen— cover their eyes, or make them turn their backs so that you can feel free to word associate without restraint. I guarantee you will be moved by your story, moved to tears, to laughter, and to revelation.

Joseph Campbell's Legacy

I was surprised to discover recently that there is a generation of young adults who don't already know about Joseph Campbell and the marvelous work he did in examining and explaining myth. Joseph Campbell, for most of his teaching life, was Professor of Literature at Sarah Lawrence College. He was a scholar with unparalleled thirst for knowledge, and the single unifying goal within his seeking was to understand mythology. Many of his lectures were recorded so that in addition to his written works, we can also enjoy the man in a lecture setting and get a taste of what his students enjoyed in the classroom. Campbell sought to explain the relevance of mythology to us personally, and in doing so he brought together the psychology of Carl Jung with archaeology, anthropology, and the mythology of the ancient worlds. If you are not already familiar with the enormous influence Campbell has had on our understanding of mythology as a psychological underpinning, then I urge you to sample his writings or his lectures.

Joseph Campbell told us that the archetypes of the unconscious are universal, though they may appear to each of our cultures within a specific context. These archetypes are universally accessible through art. From the earliest cave paintings to modern art, we understand art by means of our unconscious understanding of archetypes. We use ritual and myth to place ourselves within the active center of the story, to align ourselves within the universe. Joseph Campbell says, "Getting in harmony with the universe and then staying there is the principle function of mythology."

Mythology is the story created to explain the archetype. You've seen this as you worked through the meditations. The universal story is the guide for our own personal destiny. For a time in the middle of the last century, it was popular in philosophy to maintain a theory that the basis of all universe was chaos and that personal choice was everything, even the only thing. We might see this as the struggle to create a role for ourselves out of disorder. Campbell saw how drastically opposed this notion was to the Eastern concept of an ordered world. Western roles were indeed choices; while Eastern structure meant that each of us simply lived life, no choice. Perhaps we have worn ourselves out with all this role-playing, when in the end, all we need do is be in "dharma" purposefully living life. When I ask us to *become Hummingbird*, I am basically saying the same thing. Here is your life, your destiny, live it! Be, here, now. Be awake in this moment. To understand that life, we use our accessible archetypes to see the positive goals as well as our projected shadow selves. Hopefully, as we age, we get better and better at seeing the shadows, at rejecting fear and anger in favor of compassion and generosity.

Campbell was fond of reciting the moving, 19th century letter from Chief Seattle to the US government on the eve of his capitulation. In his letter Chief Seattle says, "Man did not weave the web of life, he is merely a strand in it. Whatever he does to the web, he does to himself." Remember these words. He is speaking of the holiness of Earth. If you create a sacred wheel with a dozen spokes, and each spoke, each thread, represents an archetype that guides you on your path, no matter where you put yourself on that wheel that is Earth, you are always connected by threads to every other part of the journey. We, as a species, have forgotten this connection. Part of the purpose of your mythology is to re-remember the story. Our story. Our connectedness. The story that was told to you before you were even born, from lifetimes ago. The story you have never heard but have always known. The story only you can tell in your own unique voice, with your own unique set of characters, threads, branches. Come to the fire and sit, and when it is your turn, take the staff in your hand, and tell the story. Place yourself firmly in the cosmos. Recognize that you have always been everywhere, and yet you are only here and now. Become Hummingbird, taste the sweet nectar of the journey, engage, defend, protect, and honor yourself and your Earth.

Afterword

Now that you've worked your way through the steps and chapters of this book—the long journey of your becoming—your perspective has changed and not just about your self. If I have shared anything with you at all, I hope it is that this universe we live in depends upon all of us to live with grace. It is no longer valid to demand something special. Every time you use the word "I" it should be done with the weight of all creatures on our planet behind it. We must live in consequence. When we speak, we must speak for the whales and we must speak for the birds. We must speak with the fearlessness of the lion and on behalf of the meekness of the lamb. If we do not live in a state of complete awareness of the fragility of our earth, we do not deserve to thrive as a species. There are no exceptions.

It has been a difficult decade since this book was first published. Climate change has made every species more vulnerable than ever before. We live in a turbulent, upside-down world. The Q'ero predict a future where this world rights itself. I hope they are right; but it is clear we are like alcoholics who haven't yet reached the bottom. If you have worked through this book, you know what you can and should be doing to help yourself and the world to evolve. Become *luminous*, please. Behave every day, take every step on the earth, speak every truth, without greed or personal agenda: live with grace. As we put this second edition to press we are in the midst of a pandemic that threatens the essence of being human and demands of us that we become luminous. Remember what I said, remember what the shaman tell us: *Evolve or die out.*

When I wrote the last chapter of this book twelve years ago, I spoke gently to you of how important it was that we bring generosity and grace to our selves and to earth's creatures. In the years since, we are seeing civil society devolve, weather extremes increase, endangered creatures disappear, flood rage, fire destroy, and pandemic bring us to our knees. There isn't any time left to coax each other gently. Each of us must live every day as if it is our last. Find grace within yourself and then turn and share it with someone in greater need. Once again, the indigenous peoples of the earth are at greatest risk, put their well-being at the top of your list. We have learned every important thing there is to know about what is sacred from them.

My own personal practice of the sacred has changed because of the knowledge shared by the Q'ero, and in the past decade it has smoothed of its own organic accord into a habit, a regime, a safety net of rituals and beliefs which nurture me and guide my everyday philosophy. I hope that upon finishing this book that you too will develop a confident ritual practice that is instinctive and not mere pantomime. Remember my story of the runaway donkey on the mountain path? The shaman with us reacted with immediate instinct. Their care, their energy of support filled all of us. They didn't need to look up a passage in a bible, they didn't need to stop and think about what spell to say. Everything they needed was a part of their whole being radiating toward the little boy and his donkey. Find your own practice, take what fits you from what I have shared, from what you already knew as right behavior, make the rituals second nature to you by their familiarity and use; and then look around you for the little boy and his donkey, and reach out. Then and only then will you have evolved.

Jane Galer
May 2020
Mendocino County, California

Additional Exercises

Ancestor Retrieval

Use this exercise to access an ancestor who will guide you through your past lives and assist you in understanding your current relationships with family members. This ancestor may not be someone you have met, or know of, and he must already be dead (sounds funny but you'd be surprised how many people want to access Uncle Harry when they could just call him up on the phone instead!) Begin as you always do, set the meditation space and prepare yourself. Don't rush, this is an important journey. You will access this ancestor repeatedly as you work through this lifetime if you have done the initial journey with care and clear intent.

A. Breathe

In your breath look inward, not into your physical self, but into your luminous body. Breathe who you really are. Breathe as a prayer. Use the act of prayer to engage the sacred. Breathe your myths, your wounds, your contracts, and promises. Who are you? Who are you becoming?

Call on all the places of power that resonate for you in this world and the other worlds, physical places that speak to you. Call on the teachers, guides, spirits, and angels, anyone who has contributed to who you are now. Breathe, and pray. When prayer comes from our deepest self, it becomes our mantra, and allows us to access and bridge all possibilities. This isn't church prayer; this is your deepest self as breath.

B. Journey

To find our past lives, we must first access the Upper world. Imagine a great tree in front of you, whose roots go deep into the earth, whose trunk is wide and spacious, and whose branches extend into the heavens. Send your luminous body into the trunk of this tree. Experience yourself within the tree, how does it feel to be held in its embrace? The sap flows through you as it rises from the roots and up into the branches. Allow the sap to carry you to the upper most branches and up, up to a place above the clouds. You are in the Upper world, on solid ground. The gatekeeper of the Upper world approaches you and asks what you desire. Tell him you wish to meet an ancestor who can guide you to your past lives.

Go with the gatekeeper and meet your ancestor. As you approach sense how your ancestor moves near you, how he or she greets you. Allow the ancestor to take you further into the Upper world beyond the clouds now into a land of crystal and golden cities that lie nestled between two green lush mountains. These are the apus, the masculine and feminine of the universe. They hold all of the information about your lifetimes. Watch your ancestor as she turns a small corner of this world into a recreation of your past life. What do you see? Who are you in this other life? What time period is it? How did you live? How did you die? Do you see your sisters or brothers there? Who were they? How were you related? What karma keeps you together in this lifetime? What lies unfinished from this other lifetime? What have you brought with you as a contract between you to this lifetime of today?

C. Return

When it is time to go your ancestor guide will lead you back from the city of crystal and gold, back down to the clouds. Before you take your leave, your ancestor guide will hand you an object. Put out your hand. What has she given you? This is your power talisman. When you have a chance, find this object in your real world and keep it near by so that when you need help in understanding your global responsibility you have a tool at hand.

Now thank your ancestor guide and bid her goodbye. Thank the gatekeeper as you cross the threshold of the Upper world. Before you descend, call on a winged spirit animal to accompany you. Sense how it drapes its wings around you, holding you sweetly. Know that it is here to guide and protect you.

With your spirit animal, go through the clouds and into the uppermost limbs of the great tree, descending down the branches as they grow thicker and thicker, allowing the sap to carry you back down through the massive trunk. Feel the spirit animal coming with you, flying around you as you descend. Step out of the tree and back into your physical body. Sense the spirit animal hovering around you. Look deeply into its eyes. What color are they? Extend your hands and take the winged animal energetically into your seventh chakra. Feel it extend its wings inside your heart.

Come back into our world, bringing forth what you have retrieved, remembering who you are, where you come from, and what you came here to experience. Carry this intent in your heart with purity and compassion.

Breathe. Open your eyes.

Record your experiences in your journal. We often forget the details of these other world journeys because they engage a different part of our brain than our normal waking consciousness. Writing down the details of your journey will enliven the experience and open up new insights as you record them as memory in your thinking brain. Journaling here is not a narcissistic endeavor; it is a part of the information transfer mechanism your brain requires in order to elucidate the experience.

Life Lines

This exercise is not for everyday, this is for the big moments in life: crises, major decisions, and passages. Did you know your lifeline changes over time? We don't want to be checking it constantly, but here's an altar exercise to do that combines life line reading with divination using Rune stones. (You will need a runic interpretation book or look online for interpreting rune images.)

By now, your altar probably has a collection of stones and artifacts that have been absorbing your life intentions. Looking at the palm of your dominant hand, recreate the lines of your palm using the stones from your altar. Choose one specific stone to represent the "you now" position along your lifeline. You are reading your palm for a specific moment in time; formulate that moment into a question. When you have the question firmly in your mind, look at the stone lines and compare the line combinations to the Runic alphabet. You will be able to pick out two or three rune images. Remember that some of them might be upside down or backwards. Copy the rune images into your journal along with your query, and then read the interpretations for each rune. How are the runes describing your current moment? What advice do you get from each rune individually? What is the progress of the combined runes?

What action can you see as required? What part can ceremony play in how you work through this problem?

I did this exercise the first time when I was confronted with an abnormality on my annual mammogram. I put my "you now" stone at the point in my lifeline where it seemed to branch: two options, one shorter path, and one longer path. I could clearly see three rune images in my palm, one front facing and two reversed. The runes confirmed two options, two paths ahead and a long journey with a successful conclusion. To conclude my work with the lifeline stones I created ceremony. I removed the short path stones and took them to my favorite place at the ocean; I called in all of my support system, my angels and guides, and the mountains, and cast the stones into the water.

When you complete your own process, thank the stones you worked with and cleanse them with incense or holy water so that they are fresh for the next mission you assign them.

Destiny Tracking
Ninth Wave Meditation

This is a destiny tracking meditation that requires a visit to an ocean beach or a large body of water that is producing waves. (Please be very aware of the power of water; never turn your back on the ocean.)

The Irish have a saying I have mentioned before. "*Do not venture beyond the ninth wave.*" Perhaps in ancient times this was wise advise, the ninth wave is just about as far out in the ocean as we should go and still be in sight of rescue. It got me thinking, about the ocean, about the horizon, about the whales and the fullness of their destiny tracking as they monitor our progress from the deep.

Choose a stone from your altar to represent you and your current destiny line. Spend some time holding it, blowing into it. Then go to the beach and stand at the edge of the water, the very edge, so that you at least some of the time feel the water lapping at your feet. Now do your breathing skills and turn your gaze to the ocean far out, about nine waves out, but don't distract yourself counting. Just find a point to look to with your meditator's way of seeing, hold the stone in your palms together, prayer pose. Don't close your eyes! Always be mindful of mamacocha, Mother Ocean.

Now when you are ready you are going to notice or track, as we would say, the next nine wave cycles as if they are a symbolic measuring device of your current destiny. It's all right if you count one or two more or one less, don't focus all your attention on counting waves or you will busy your mind too much to notice their quality. What is each wave like? Where does it come from? Does it lap gently at your toes, or did it nearly knock you off your feet? Which waves were strongest, the first ones which represent the immediate situation? Or the middle cycle, which might mean some time a few years from now? How did the ninth wave come? In a rush? What else did you notice? Are you alone or is there a crowd on the beach with you? Did the waves consistently try to knock you off your feet? I was amazed to find that there are many types of waves; while sometimes they came down along the shoreline, others crashed and broke at my ankles, nearly knocking me off my feet. What event did this represent? Perhaps the side waves represented a sudden shift I wouldn't see coming. What was it that threatened to knock me off my path? When you have counted nine waves, blow into your stone again and cast it into the sea, thanking it for allowing you this look at the destiny you now own. Step back to the safety of the shore, and spend some time writing in your journal about what your tracking showed you. Are there places in your life to come that you would like to change? Think about how you can effect change about a lifeline that has not yet occurred.

Altered States Simulation

Scientists are writing widely these days about the details of chemically altered states of consciousness. As scientists compulsively do, they are identifying stages and methods and ways of gaining access to the dimensions that most of us do not work in on a day-to-day basis. Some indigenous shaman use plant medicine to achieve an altered state, and many Western shaman have adopted this method as well, while others use tone vibrations to cue the brain, and others simply meditate their way across the bridge. If we ask these shaman what it looks like they pretty much agree on a basic three-part experience. In the first part, the beginning of the trance, many shaman recount seeing geometric shapes, stars, and squiggles, and things that look rather like DNA. In the second, they often conjure frightening animals, usually snakes (also curiously like DNA, aren't they?), and in the third and deepest stage, they usually have an encounter with an otherworld being in order to exchange important information.

This little experiment simulates the early state of trance and it's fun to see where you can take it from there. The process serves to show you the physical brain response which distracts from worrying about whether the trance will work or not, and may if you allow yourself to, merge into at least the second stage. What we are doing is playing with light and the retinal responses of our eye, and thus our brains, but it's a window into what a shaman sees in a hallucinogenic trance.

At night, and from complete darkness, turn on a flashlight and watch something out your window, doesn't matter what, for a few minutes. Then turn off the flashlight, close your eyes, and enjoy the fireworks. (Don't shine the flashlight into your eyes! Point it away from you.)

Bibliography

Books about the Shaman's Path

Andrews, Ted. *Animal Speak, The Spiritual and Magical Powers of Creatures Great & Small.* MN: Llewellyn Publications, 2005.

———. *Animal-Wise, The Spirit Language and Signs of Nature.* TN: Dragonhawk Publishing, 1999.

Arrien, Angeles. *The Four-Fold Way, Walking the Paths of the Warrior, Teacher, Healer and Visionary.* San Francisco: Harper One, 1993.

Bowlby, Jo. *A Book For Life: 10 steps to spiritual wisdom, a clear mind and lasting happiness.* London:Yellow Kite, 2021.

Heaven, Ross & Howard G. Charing. *Plant Spirit Shamanism, Traditional Techniques for Healing the Soul.* VT: Destiny Books, 2006

Matthews, John & Caitlin. *Walkers Between the Worlds, The Western Mysteries from Shaman to Magus.* VT: Inner Traditions Publishing, 2003.

MacEowen, Frank. *The Mist-Filled Path.* VT: New World Library, 2002.

Rasmussen, Jon. *Dreaming Your World into Being, The Shaman's Secrets to Having the Life You Desire Now.* Booksurge Publishing, 2008.

Villoldo, Alberto. *Shaman, Healer, Sage: How to Heal Yourself and Others with the Energy Medicine of the Americas.* NY: Harmony Books, 2000.

———. *The Four Insights: Wisdom, Power and Grace of the Earthkeepers.* CA: Hay House, Inc., 2006.

Books about Archetypes and Mythology

Classical:

Arrien, Angeles. *The Nine Muses, A Mythological Path to Creativity.* Tarcher/ Putnam. 2000.

Aycock, Wendell M. and Theodore M. Klein, eds. *Classical Mythology in Twentieth-century Thought and Literature.* Texas Tech University Press. 1980.

Greene, Liz and Juliet Sharman-Burke. *The Mythic Journey, The Meaning of Myth as a Guide for Life.* NY: Fireside Books, Simon and Schuster, 2000.

Morford, Mark and Robert J. Lenardon. *Classical Mythology. 6th edition.* NY: Longman, 1999.

World:

Campbell, Joseph. *Creative Mythology, The Masks of God.* NY: Penguin/ Compass, 1998.

———. *Pathways to Bliss, Mythology and Personal Transformation.* CA: New World Library, 2004.

Karlsdottir, Alice. *Magic of the Norse Goddesses.* Runa/Raven Press, 2003.

Matthews, Caitlin. *Sophia: Goddess of Wisdom, Bride of God. revised edition.* IL: Quest Books, Theosophical Press, 2001.

Willis, Roy, ed. *World Mythology. The Illustrated Guide.* UK: Oxford University Press, 2006.

Celtic/Britain:

Byatt, A.S. *Elementals, Stories of Fire and Ice.* Vintage Books, 2000.

trans. Gantz, Jeffrey. *The Mabinogion.* Penguin Classics, 1996.

Matthews, Caitlin. *King Arthur and The Goddess of the Land. The Divine Feminine in the Maginogion.* VT: Inner Traditions, 2002.

———. *Mabon and the Guardians of Celtic Britain. Hero Myths in the Mabinogion.* VT: Inner Traditions, 2002.

Rolleston, T.W. *Myths and Legends of the Celtic Race.* London: Constable, 1985.

Books about Tarot

Arrien, Angeles. *The Tarot Handbook, Practical Applications of Ancient Visual Symbols.* NY: Tarcher/Putnam, 1997.

Black, Kat. *Golden Tarot.* CT: US Games Systems, 2003.

Carr-Gomm, Philip and Stephanie. *The Druidcraft Tarot.* NY: St Martin's Press, 2004.

Di Vicenzo, Sofia. *Sola Busca Tarot.* CT: US Games Systems, Inc, 1998.

Huson, Paul. *Mystical Origins of the Tarot. From Ancient Roots to Modern Usage.* VT: Destiny Books, 2004.

Matthews, Caitlin. *The Celtic Wisdom Tarot.* VT: Destiny Books, 1999.

Place, Robert M. *The Tarot, History, Symbolism, and Divination.* Tarcher/Penguin, 2005.

Books about symbols and mythology in art

Cooper, J.C. *An Illustrated Encyclopedia of Traditional Symbols.* London: Thames & Hudson, 1978.

Roob, Alexander. *Alchemy & Mysticism.* London: Taschen, 2006.

various editors: *The Guide to Imagery Series.* J. Paul Getty Museum, Los Angeles. including: *Gods and Heroes in Art, Angels and Demons in Art* etc.

Books about Psychology

Banzhaf, Hajo. *Tarot and the Journey of the Hero.* ME: Weiser, Inc., 2000.

Myss, Caroline. *Sacred Contracts.* NY: Three Rivers Press. Random House, 2002.

Rosengarten, Arthur. *Tarot and Psychology, Spectrums of Possibility.* MN: Paragon House, 2000.

Ryan, Robert E. *Shamanism and the Psychology of C.G. Jung.* UK: Vega, 2002.

Von Franz, Marie-Louise. *The Interpretation of Fairy Tales.* revised edition. UK: Shambala, 1996.

Practicing Shaman & Teachers:

Jo Bowlby - jobowlby.com. UK based coach, mentor, shaman, Amazon and Andes trips

John & Karen Cantwell - Slí an Chroi, Dublin Ireland, Celtic shamanism workshops, training, calendar ceremonial events

Linda L. Fitch - lindalfitch.com. shaman, coach, mentor, trips to Amazon and Andes, online & in person classes, lectures, meditations

Jon Rasmussen - shamanjon.com. coach, mentor, shaman, virtual and in person consultation

Wake and Kinlen Wheeler -Sacred Pathways Eugene, OR., shaman, consultants, trips to sites worldwide, online store, ceremonial gatherings

Author's Biography

Jane Galer holds a BA in philosophy, an MA in material culture studies, and an Advanced Certificate in museum curation for archaeologists. She studied with the Q'ero shaman of the Peruvian High Andes with The Four Winds Society for three years culminating in on-site individual work in the Sacred Valley of Peru. She has been given the rites of a full mesa-carrying shaman in the Q'ero tradition and studied with the shaman and druids of Celtic Ireland and Brittany. As a shaman, she is a ceremonial specialist and keeper of wisdom and tradition. Jane is first and foremost a poet, as well as an author and polymath whose interests range from shamanism to prehistoric British and European archaeology to genetic genealogy. Her work includes three volumes of poetry, the novel *The Navigator's Wife*, and *Spirit Dogs: How to Be Your Dog's Personal Shaman*. She is working on a new collection of annotated poems titled *Forward & in the Dark*. Jane was born in Illinois but spent seven formative years living in Iran and Lebanon. She has lived all fifty years of her married life in northern California where she now lives on the remote north coast with her husband and dog, Tweed.

www.janegaler.com

Printed in the USA
CPSIA information can be obtained
at www.ICGtesting.com
CBHW081152150624
10061CB00004B/40